More Praise for *Humble Consultin*

"In this book, Ed Schein has looked bac
consulting experience and come up
who are called upon to give help or advice, be they boss, consultant,
parent, or friend, should start by reading this."

—Charles Handy, author of *The Age of Unreason*

"Chock-full of useful case examples, *Humble Consulting* is about
establishing a relationship with the client that is collaborative, personal, and empathetic rather than prescriptive. Schein has once
again contributed significantly and creatively to our field of organization change and development."

—W. Warner Burke, PhD, E. L. Thorndike Professor of Psychology and
    Education, Teachers College, Columbia University, and Editor, *Journal*
    of Applied Behavioral Science

"Ed Schein's books on consulting have always been the most professionally useful things I read. And this book could once again reshape
the consulting industry. It shifts the place from which effective consultants operate from the head to the heart and from the heart to the
hand. Essential reading!"

—Otto Scharmer, Senior Lecturer, MIT, cofounder of the U.Lab, and
    author of *Theory U*

"*Humble Consulting* pulls the curtain back on the pretense that the vast
majority of consultants and consulting organizations put forward—that
they have 'the answer.' I plan on keeping a copy in my office to hand
out to consultants as they continue to show up and ask that I tell them
what keeps me up at night and they respond with the solution that
they uniquely have to address it."

—James Hereford, Chief Operating Officer, Stanford Health Care

"Long a critic of OD's overreliance on process, I've always admired Ed
Schein's insistence that process consultation be relevant. Now, in his
new book, *Humble Consulting*, he shows us how. In his usual and
clear style, he calls OD practitioners to account and to help in powerful and integrated ways."

—Chris Worley, Professor and Strategy Director, NEOMA Business
    School Center for Leadership and Effective Organizations

"In *Humble Consulting*, master consultant Edgar Schein shows us
how to escape the limitations of a traditional consulting practice to

vastly improve both the impact and the meaning of our work. This book is at once brilliant and incredibly practical."
   —Anthony L. Suchman, MD, MA, consultant, Relationship Centered
      Health Care

"*Humble Consulting* is a book every leader and every consultant should read. Using numerous cases from his own experience, Schein describes the specific components of a true helping relationship and shows the powerful impact when consulting rests on curious questioning that honors and unlocks the knowledge held by the other."
   —David L. Bradford, PhD, Eugene D. O'Kelly Senior Lecturer in Leadership,
      Emeritus, Stanford University Graduate School of Business, and coauthor
      of the bestselling books *Influence without Authority* and *Power Up*

"Finally, a consulting process that demonstrates and emulates the type of culture toward which organizations and their leaders aspire."
   —Robert Cooke, author of Human Synergistics' Organizational Culture
      Inventory

"Ed Schein once again moves the needle in refining the essence of consulting. Schein invokes a shift from considering clients as objects to considering clients as living, dynamic beings. The artistry of balancing formality and intimacy, dancing with the dynamic client system, paying attention to the environment, and engaging in endless reflective learning makes for a potent model and process."
   —Sarita Chawla, President, Metalens Consulting; Senior Faculty, New
      Ventures West; and Diamond Approach teacher

"In *Humble Consulting*, Ed Schein weaves the cultural and process consulting threads of his life's work into a masterpiece of emotional, cultural, and methodological insight. Read this book and be prepared to change your mind, heart, and practice."
   —David E. Goldberg, author of *The Design of Innovation* and coauthor
      of *A Whole New Engineer*

"This senior icon in the field continues to make meaningful and significant contributions that could only be realized through years of experience and reflection. I have been reading Edgar Schein's work for almost fifty years now, and I have learned from each of his works. But somehow, this, his latest, is special."
   —Peter F. Sorensen, PhD, Director, Master of Science in Management
      and Organizational Behavior program, Benedictine University

Humble Consulting

Humble Consulting

How to Provide Real Help Faster

EDGAR H. SCHEIN

Berrett–Koehler Publishers, Inc.
a BK Business book

Berrett-Koehler Publishers, Inc.
1333 Broadway, Suite 1000
Oakland, CA 94612-1921
Tel: (510) 817-2277 | Fax: (510) 817-2278 | www.bkconnection.com

Ordering Information
Quantity sales. Special discounts are available on quantity purchases by corporations, associations, and others. For details, contact the "Special Sales Department" at the Berrett-Koehler address above.
Individual sales. Berrett-Koehler publications are available through most bookstores. They can also be ordered directly from Berrett-Koehler: Tel: (800) 929-2929; Fax: (802) 864-7626; www.bkconnection.com.
Orders for college textbook/course adoption use. Please contact Berrett-Koehler: Tel: (800) 929-2929; Fax: (802) 864-7626.

Distributed to the U.S. trade and internationally by Penguin Random House Publisher Services.

Berrett-Koehler and the BK logo are registered trademarks of Berrett-Koehler Publishers, Inc.

Printed in the United States of America.

Berrett-Koehler books are printed on long-lasting acid-free paper. When it is available, we choose paper that has been manufactured by environmentally responsible processes. These may include using trees grown in sustainable forests, incorporating recycled paper, minimizing chlorine in bleaching, or recycling the energy produced at the paper mill.

Library of Congress Cataloging-in-Publication Data
Names: Schein, Edgar H., author.
Title: Humble consulting : how to provide real help faster / Edgar H. Schein.
Description: Oakland, CA : Berrett-Koehler Publishers, Inc., [2016] | "A B-K Business book." | Includes bibliographical references.
Identifiers: LCCN 2015045587 | ISBN 9781626567207 (pbk.).
Subjects: LCSH: Business consultants. | Consultants.
Classification: LCC HD69.C6 S278 2016 | DDC 001—dc23 LC record available at http://lccn.loc.gov/2015045587

First Edition

23 22 21 20 19 18 | 10 9 8 7 6 5 4 3

Produced and designed by BookMatters, edited by Mike Mollett, proofed by Janet Blake, indexed by Leonard Rosenbaum, and cover designed by Susan Malikowski, DesignLeaf Studio

I dedicate this book to my late wife, Mary,
who practiced humble consulting
long before I realized its importance.

Contents

Preface

This book brings together various insights and ideas I have acquired over fifty years of research, teaching, and consulting and, at the same time, reflects how the kinds of problems that organizations face in our rapidly changing world have forced the evolution of those ideas.

As I began my career as a human relations trainer and part-time consultant in the 1960s, I evolved the model of Process Consultation (introduced in my books *Process Consultation*, 1969; and *Process Consultation Revisited*, 1999), which emphasizes the need to involve the client in the process of figuring out what is wrong and what can be done about it. After several decades of working with this model and updating the book, I began to realize that the model we were using for organization and management consulting really had broader applications to all kinds of helping relationships, resulting in the 2009 book *Helping*. Analyzing the helping process from a sociological point of view also revealed how much our cultural norms influenced what we thought should be both the client's role and the consultant's role in the helping process.

In my own experience as a helper, it seemed crucial that the client really be able to tell what is bothering him or her and be able to be open and trusting in doing so. I then discovered that the major inhibiting factor to clients' being open and trusting is the cultural force in the United States toward *telling* as being the heroic model, which led helping and consulting models to be structured in terms of the formal professional stages of *diagnose* and then *tell as recommendations*. My management consulting friends told me that "this is required if you are really doing your job," which, to my dismay, I found many clients passively believed.

I recognized that the obsession with *telling* was a broader characteristic of the US managerial culture, which led me to write the book *Humble Inquiry* (2013) to point out how much potential harm was done in making subordinates feel psychologically unsafe in *upward reporting* if they saw safety or quality issues in how work was getting done.

In my own consulting efforts, I found that telling did not work and, furthermore, that the clients who called me in for consultation often had previously experienced the formal approach with other consultants and did not find the *diagnose and then recommend* approach terribly helpful. The formal process often missed the real problem or recommended things that could not be implemented for a variety of reasons that the consultant evidently had not considered.

At the same time, the problems that confronted leaders and managers became more complex to diagnose and even more difficult to "fix." I also learned through several experiences that will be discussed in the cases in this book that sometimes just the earliest questions, comments, and puzzlements that I expressed in the *initial* contacts with a client proved to be very helpful in enabling the client to perceive and think about the situation. This often led to immediate next moves that the client could think of that were seen by both helper and client as immediately beneficial.

All this led me to go beyond the previous models and write about what I experienced—real help can be fast, but it requires an open, trusting relationship with the client that the helper has to build from the very beginning. Because of the difficulty and complexity of the problems, and because the client's own view of what is going on is so important in the relationship, this also requires a great deal of humility in the consultant. So in this book I will describe the new kinds of problems, the new consultant–client relationship that will have to be built, and the new kinds of attitudes and behaviors that consultants will have to learn in order to be really helpful.

I think of this as an evolution in my thinking. Many of these ideas may have been implicit in earlier works, but they are only now coming into consciousness both as insights and as new principles of what has to happen if we really want to help on complex, dynamic "messy" problems and if we want to do it fast because, in many cases, clients need to do something adaptive right away.

Where Does This Fit into a Larger Historical Context?

Humble Consulting draws on elements of many prior models that deal with complexity, interdependence, diversity, and instability. Almost every theory of helping refers to the concept of *relationship*, but few of them talk about *levels* of relationships and what is involved in negotiating them. One exception is Otto Scharmer's *Theory U* (2007), in which he explicitly differentiates levels of conversation in his analysis of how to reach the deepest level within ourselves and in our relationships to find the true sources of innovation.

The theories and models that are most relevant to understanding these kinds of problems and developing workable *next moves* were initially best articulated in the study of highly reliable organizations by Karl Weick with his concepts of "loose coupling," "sense making," "embracing errors," and "resilience" (Weick and Sutcliffe, 2007). On the sociological side, I have always found Erving Goffman's analysis of interaction and "situational proprieties" to be an essential model for understanding how relationships are formed, maintained, and repaired when damaged (Goffman, 1959, 1963, 1967).

Closely related are the systemic models of "organizational learning" (e.g., Senge, 1990) and family therapy (e.g., Madanes, 1981). The work on "mindfulness" (Langer, 1997) is crucial in what I see to be the new skills that will be needed. The change programs that rely on so-called lean methods, based on the work of Deming and Juran that evolved into the Toyota Production System, are relevant if they are well executed and involve the employees who actually do the work (Plsek, 2014). Open sociotechnical systems approaches to problem identification and solution as evolved by the Tavistock Clinic have provided much more helpful ideas than standardized methods of measurement, analysis, and problem solving.

Perhaps most relevant of all is what Bushe and Marshak (2015) have identified in the last decade as "*dialogic* organization development," as contrasted with "*diagnostic* organization development," in highlighting what leadership theorists like Heifetz (1994) also emphasize—that the complex problems of today are not technical ones that can be solved with specific tools. The best we can do is to find workable responses or what I am calling here "adaptive moves." This will involve new kinds of conversations of a more dialogic, open-ended variety. The emphasis on the concept of "moves" is important in this context because it implies action without necessarily having a plan or solution in mind.

In the end I fall back on much of my learning in running sensitivity training groups in human relations labs for the National Training Labs in Bethel, Maine, where the key operational concept was "spirit of inquiry" and accepting that we did not always know where our learning process would take us (Schein and Bennis, 1965). Building a relationship that enables the client to "learn how to learn" was then and becomes now more than ever one of the crucial goals of Humble Consulting.

The spirit of inquiry is best exemplified nowadays in the concept of "dialogue" as propounded by Bill Isaacs (1999) and in Barrett's hugely insightful book *Yes to the Mess* (2012), which shows us brilliantly how the skills of improvisation as exhibited in the jazz combo provide some of the most important clues as to what helpers and leaders will have to be able to do in the future.

How the Book Is Organized

Chapter 1 lays out the basic problem—the complex messy problems of today and the future require a new model of helping, coaching, and consultation. Chapter 2 lays out the new elements or components of the model of Humble Consulting. The following chapters then explain and exemplify each of those components. Chapter 3 explains the concept of a Level Two relationship. Chapter 4 shows how that relationship has to be built from the moment of first contact with the client by adopting a certain attitude that hinges on maximizing curiosity. Chapter 5 explores the whole concept of *personalization* as key to the new consulting model. Chapter 6 highlights that the consulting is almost always more helpful on the *processes* that occur between client and consultant as they explore how to make adaptive moves. Chapter 7 then explores the concept of *adaptive moves* in more detail and in terms of the innovations that are required to make them helpful. The book closes with some conclusions and challenges for the future.

ONE

I Am the Consultant, and I Don't Know What to Do!

I have had a monthly lunch meeting with a group of senior executives and doctors from a large hospital and medical school that are both part of a large academic medical complex. We meet to see how the hospital and medical school can further improve the quality of medical care, patient and employee safety, patient experiences in the hospital, research breakthroughs, and medical education. I have learned that the doctor community includes clinicians, researchers, and teachers who have different ultimate agendas, yet they have to coordinate their efforts and are all dependent on the same sources of financial support from the hospital and the university.

The hospital is the primary source of income for the medical school and for some of the research. The administrators, who may or may not be doctors, have to apportion funds between the needs of research, clinical practice, safety, maintenance, expansion of the delivery system in the community, and a reserve for future building projects. The doctors are all employed by the medical school, but if they are clinicians in the hospital, they also report to the hospital administrators. The senior administrators are working hard at getting everyone on the same page while recognizing that the goals of research, education, and clinical practice are to some degree different, that the individuals pursuing these goals have different personal agendas, and that their leaders are protective of those goals and agendas.

I have been invited to join this group because of my work on organizational culture, my experience as a process consultant, and my growing interest in health care and hospital administration. Over the past several years, I have also met other hospital administrators as part of a small think tank and have learned that this set of problems is shockingly common in large university-based medical centers.

As I approach tomorrow's lunch, I realize that I don't know what to do!

My Reflection on This Situation

Over my many years of consulting, I have from time to time found that being the expert and providing information and/ or advice works, but only for simple, bounded problems. I have also played "doctor" to organizational clients by doing diagnoses and delivering recommendations. That has worked only occasionally, when I happened to have enough insider information about the organization's identity, mission, and cultural DNA to be able to make suggestions that would be implementable.

I learned early on to be what I called a "process consultant," someone who would help a group in the organization do more effectively what it needed to do in terms of its basic function and mission. That usually involved getting into a relationship with the client that would enable us to figure out together what was wrong and how to fix it. But that process also failed if the problem was complex, culturally multifaceted, and constantly changing. To deal with my medical lunch group, I needed yet another way to think about how to be helpful in the face of such complexity and rapid change.

I then thought about the implications of a case that happened a few years ago that I call "my most successful consultation on the perplexing problem of how to change culture."

CASE 1. Culture Change in Beta Power Company

Potential client on the phone: *Hello, Dr. Schein, this is Sue Jones from the Beta Power Company. I am the head of HR and Management Development. Our new CEO asked me to call you to find out if you would be willing to come and help us change what we have discovered to be a rigid, stodgy formal culture. It is hard to get any new programs going because we keep running into these old traditions and ways of doing things. Would you come visit our company to learn more and help us launch some culture change programs?*

(As I listened to this proposal and question, I sensed two main reactions in me. First, it sounded interesting and was certainly within the range of the types of projects that I felt I could tackle successfully. But, second, I recalled having had some bad experiences visiting organizations without knowing more, and especially without knowing what the new CEO actually had in mind in what he called "a rigid, stodgy culture." I also wanted a little more information about the motivation of the CEO. Was he just going to have Sue Jones do this? Or would he involve himself, which would be crucial if culture change was to happen. These thoughts led to the following conversation, which I call *personalization*.)

Ed S.: *That sounds interesting and could be complicated. I think it might be important to talk about this with the CEO away from the company to explore what is going on and what he has in mind. Do you think he would be willing to talk with me separately and maybe visit me in Cambridge?*

(This response was the first of what I call *adaptive moves* to begin to build a more personal relationship with the client to find out what is really on his mind.)

S. J.: *You are right that we maybe need to talk this through away from the company, so let me explore with him the possibility of coming to see you. I'll get back in touch.*

(A week later.)

S. J.: *I spoke to our CEO, and he was quite enthusiastic about coming to visit you. He will bring his new COO as well, and I will be accompanying them. So when can we set a date for a half-day meeting?*

Ed S.: *Here are some dates to check out. Also, I presume it is understood that I will be billing you for this half day.*

(I had learned from other experiences that sometimes the best help occurs in the early meetings, so I would bill for those early meetings unless it was clearly a short exploratory phone call, lunch, or visit.)

S. J.: *That sounds good. We will let you know which date.*

(We met two weeks later in the garden at my house at 9 a.m. I chose to meet at my house to provide a setting that could involve food and drinks, and was therefore an invitation to personalize the situation.)

Ed S.: *Welcome! Let's talk about what is on your mind about this "rigid, stodgy culture."*

CEO: *OK, Ed. May I call you Ed?*

Ed S.: *Sure.*

CEO: *When John* [the COO] *and I began to try to implement some new programs in the company, we kept finding old habits and traditions that people seemed to want to hold on to, like the culture has kind of fossilized.*

Ed S.: *Can you give me an example?*

> (This is almost always a good thing to ask because at this point I have no idea at all what they are talking about, what their concept of culture is, or what is actually bothering them. No sooner had I asked this than John sat up in his chair and jumped into the conversation with great intensity.)

COO: *Yes, Ed, I can give you a great example that just happened yesterday. I have a staff group of about fifteen people with whom I meet regularly in this big conference room, and they always sit in the same seats. Okay, so yesterday we met, and there were only five of them there, and they again sat in those same seats,* ***even though that meant they were scattered all over the room!***

> (John looked at me expectantly, opened his hands in a gesture of "see what I am up against," and paused. At this moment I was overwhelmed by my curiosity and impulsively gave in to it without considering the possible consequences. Ask yourself what you might have done at this moment.)

Ed S. (with intensity): ***What did you do?***

COO: ***My god, I didn't do anything . . .***

(There was a long pause during which I think the CEO, the COO, and Sue all had the same insight. Here we had the top two executives of the organization complaining about stodgy subordinate behavior and asking an outsider to help them "change the culture." Somehow it had not occurred to them that their passivity was tacitly condoning the "cultural behavior" they were complaining about. I was reminded of the sage comment "You get what you settle for.")

We spent the rest of the morning listing all the actions that they could take that would send a clear signal to the organization that behavioral changes had to be made. I referred them to my *Organizational Culture and Leadership* (4th ed., 2010) in which a whole chapter discusses how executives can influence culture. At this point I felt quite comfortable playing "doctor" and recommending something. We agreed that the only further thing I should do is to check in with them every few weeks by phone to see how things were going. The CEO called me regularly over the next few months and occasionally sent me e-mails describing actions he was thinking about to get my reactions. I billed him for my time spent and provided further suggestions as needed. I did not visit or launch any formal culture projects. None were needed. I had helped them see how they could manage the culture change perfectly well on their own.

LESSONS

■ The help that they got was not connected in any **logical** way to what I had done. There was no diagnosis, no analysis, no prescription. I had no idea that my impulsive question would reframe their problem as one that they could deal with themselves. I had resisted various diagnostic questions such as "How did you feel about that," or "Why do you think they always sat in their same seats," and instead I had **given in to my curiosity.** They were delighted to have a way of moving forward that did not involve a complicated diagnostic period followed by a complicated change program. The real problem was not the stodgy culture but their own behavioral paralysis; the presented problem might have taken months to unravel, while the real problem led to an immediate adaptive move.

- My important "intervention" was to invite them to my house and ask them to "give me an example," to personalize and get a more specific sense of what was going on. What was driving me was a mixture of curiosity and commitment to being helpful.

- Focusing directly on "culture" did not seem to lead anywhere, whereas focusing on their own behavior revealed what the client actually wanted to accomplish. They did not want to know about their culture. They wanted to **change** it. A culture analysis would have been a waste of time and possibly would have distracted them from steps that they could take immediately to solve the problem that motivated them to come to a consultant in the first place.

The Paradox of Messy Complexity and Fast Help

This case taught me that *help can happen fast.* But you need to find out what is really on the client's mind and honor your own curiosity. Complex messes like the one at the university-based medical school and hospital did not lend themselves to such fast help but did illustrate that adaptive moves could be helpful. My experience with similar messes occurred in a variety of organizations with which I've had long-term relationships. In those cases, as in the problems I am encountering with clients now, the mess only emerges as initial moves are made that reveal deeper layers of issues and concerns. For example,

■ I worked with Digital Equipment Corporation (DEC) on and off for thirty years, which involved primarily helping the founder Ken Olsen deal with whatever was on his mind and working with various members of senior management as I got drawn into the daily operations of this organization. Some help happened very fast, as we will see, and, sadly, some needed help was never provided.

■ For more than ten years I worked with ConEdison, the utility that supplies the greater New York area with electric power, gas, and steam. They are operating an old system that requires careful and continuous maintenance to avoid accidents that can be deadly to the public and to their own employees. They are also responsible for maintaining a clean and safe environment under conditions of changing seasons and changing weather. I worked with senior management and the vice president of Health, Environment, and Safety to help them maintain safety in a complex, unionized, highly technical environment in which limited resources were fought over for much-needed maintenance and new improvements while the public, the regulators, and the environmental watchdogs totally mistrusted the company's efforts because of events a decade or more earlier. A similar scenario is playing out in Pacific Gas and Electric, with similar levels of complexity.

■ I encountered closely related problems in my five years
of working with INPO (the Institute of Nuclear Power
Operations) as part of an advisory board to help that
organization in its mission of assessing and aiding the
104 individual nuclear plants operating in the United
States. INPO had the problem of how to help plants maintain an absolutely safe environment under different technological, economic, and political conditions because the
power companies had complex sites that included coal-
fired and nuclear plants. The nuclear plants experienced
rapidly changing technology while they were losing technical talent as the alumni of Admiral Rickover's nuclear
submarine organization retired. Nuclear safety is highly
regulated, which creates the paradoxical reality that
the enforcement of legal, technical, and bureaucratic
standards often gets in the way of building the open and
trusting relationships that are needed and always men-
tioned as integral to "safety culture."

■ I worked for five years with the Swiss-German chemical
company Ciba-Geigy. In working on various strategic
and operational issues, I learned some powerful lessons
about organizational and national culture and saw many
complex messes, some of which were ultimately resolved
by the merger of Ciba-Geigy with Sandoz into what is
today Novartis. One messy problem that occurred in
this and in another pharmaceutical company was the
tension between basic research on the origins of disease
and applied research on developing pharmaceuticals
that cure or at least alleviate the symptoms. Aligning
basic research on the causes of diseases with applied
research on curative drugs under different sets of rules
in different countries leads to value differences on
what is "good research" that can be trusted when done

in different countries. Can basic researchers, applied researchers, practitioners, and administrators find common goals and work together, or are the occupational differences culturally too diverse?

■ I was a board member of Massachusetts Audubon Society, the major land conservation and environmental steward in New England. Some of the most interesting helping challenges in my six years there occurred when fundamental strategic questions interacted with the constraints of local community values, legal issues, lack of funds, and limitations of what the organization could actually accomplish. For example, should they support the building of windmills in the waters around Cape Cod, given that this was good for energy conservation but potentially bad for birds and fish?

Current problems that have been brought to me reflect growing complexity around coordination between silos, between functions, and between cultural units. For example, a CEO wants a better process for hiring researchers to overcome the following "problem": while the principal investigators are still waiting for the grant money, they are pressuring the human resources function to begin to advertise for the needed research jobs, leading to promises of employment that occasionally cannot be honored because the research money did not come through, resulting in both embarrassment and lawsuits.

A hospital system that has units all over the country wants to standardize certain medical processes, only to discover great resistance from several regional units that have developed strong cultures of their own and believe that their local processes are better.

A successful theater company specializing in Shakespeare

finds its market shifting because of the audience's desire for more contemporary productions while, at the same time, it is running out of money. The presenting problem is that the management neither wants to nor knows how to innovate.

What I am trying to convey in these examples is the complexity and ambiguity of figuring out what to do if we are asked to help. Sometimes the best and fastest help will be to enable the client to understand that very complexity and recognize that small adaptive moves will have to replace big diagnoses and interventions.

Why Are Problems Messier These Days?

As I reflect on this question, several forces acting together seem to be involved:

1. All the technical fields that have to collaborate have themselves become *more complex*. What this means is that the specialists working in those fields are more likely to create an occupational culture to distinguish themselves and get more benefits for their specialty.

2. The groups that have to interact and collaborate are not only more *occupationally diverse* but they now often include national cultures that have different languages and different assumptions about how things are and how things are supposed to be.

3. Greater occupational and national diversity within a given organization makes goal congruence more difficult to achieve. We all agree that the easiest way to "solve" these problems is to get everyone on the same page, bring all the "chiefs" together in the same room, and get them to agree on a single goal that everyone can relate to and support. Unfortunately, getting the right people in

the same room is usually the hardest part of this pseu-dosolution, and, even if we do, there is no guarantee that they will want to reach any kind of consensus because of deep differences in tacit cultural assumptions and goals. All the wonderful organization development processes that we advocate, like team building, scenario planning, future search, appreciative inquiry, lean production systems, and rapid prototyping, tend to assume that the people who have to agree to coordinate can be gotten to even talk to one another, much less agree on anything.

4. There isn't enough time, or at least we perceive that there isn't. Things are moving too fast to build trusting relationships, to get to know one another, to even eat together or have fun together. Getting two cultures to interact takes time. Getting three or more to interact takes more time. Speeding up processes such as going to one of the many models of rapid prototyping might work if we have figured out which process to prototype and gotten people into them that can communicate with one another. All too often we prototype the wrong process.

5. The problems that have to be addressed are not stable. The two things that are new and different about these kinds of problems is that they do not have a technical solution, and they are deeply intertwined with funda-mental strategic and structural issues *in an unstable environment*. In an unstable environment, when an organization attempts to make sense of a given situation at time 1, any interventions produce unknown effects that change the nature of the problem at time 2 and require brand-new sense-making efforts.

6. Finally, the concept of *client* will change as well in that the various individuals or groups with whom I am talk-

ing see themselves as part of a system rather than as individual clients. I may be coaching an individual executive in a key role, but it becomes immediately clear that what worries her has implications for others in the organization so that the problem formulation has to be systemic and that whatever adaptive moves are considered have to take into account the systemic consequences which, paradoxically, may be unknown.

The Need for a New Model

We are dealing with new complex problems, new kinds of client systems, and a new sense of urgency in our clients. We therefore need a new consulting model—Humble Consulting (HC). This model will tell you what attitude to strike with your clients, how to respond to their very first inquiry, and will help you to accept that initially you might not know what to do. HC is a totally different way of relating to your clients. HC presumes that you are *committed* to being helpful, bring a great deal of honest *curiosity,* and have the right *caring* attitude, a willingness to find out what is really on the client's mind.

You will then approach your first contact with that potential client with the intention of building an open and trusting relationship, and you will know that this more personal relationship will lead not only to finding out what is really on the client's mind but also to discovering whether you can help in the traditional expert or doctor role. And, paradoxically, you will discover that the relationship-building process itself leads you to behavior that the client may find immediately helpful. What you decide to do, how you will react, will *not* be big diagnoses or interventions but small adaptive moves.

The essence of that relationship-building process will be

to get past the formality of *professional distance*. Either you or the client will have to personalize the process by asking a personal question or revealing something personal. You will have to make yourself somewhat vulnerable. What exactly you will ask or reveal will depend on the situation and who the parties are, but commitment, curiosity, and caring will guide you.

Humble Consulting is new in several respects. In the next chapter, we look at this in more detail.

TWO

What Is New in Humble Consulting?

The Humble Consulting model is new in several respects. In this chapter I will review the elements of this new model briefly. The rest of the book examines each new element in greater detail with the aid of illustrative case examples from my own experience. I refer mostly to *consulting*, but the ideas apply as well to other forms of helping such as coaching, counseling, and broader organization development projects.

HC Requires a New Kind of Personal Relationship with the Client

I said early on that the consultant should have a "relationship" with the client, but I never specified what I meant by that or what kind of relationship it should be. In working on messier problems and trying to get at what is really on the client's mind and what is worrying him, I have found that the formal professional relationship that most models advocate will not get me there. I have to overcome "professional distance" and develop what I am calling a "Level Two relationship" that is more personal, more trusting, and more open.

In my book *Helping* (2009), I noted that asking for help is itself difficult in our culture, so potential clients feel "one down" and therefore not very open or trusting in their initial contact with the consultant. In the new role, the consultant must find a way to begin the personalization process from the very first encounter with the client to signal that she can be trusted and that it is safe to be more open with her. What I mean by "relationship" and Level Two will be explained in detail in Chapter 3.

The building of such a relationship begins from the moment of the first encounter, which means that the consultant must approach that initial encounter with an entirely different kind of initial behavior.

HC Requires a New Kind of Behavior in the Very First Contact

No matter what the client's initial presentation might be, building the new relationship requires that I take a helping stance and try to personalize the conversation from the moment I am in contact with the potential client, whether this is on the phone or in an e-mail or in a first meeting over lunch. I am not there to scout or diagnose or develop a contract with the client; I am there to help in whatever way I can. If what I hear totally turns me off or asks me to do something that I can't or won't do, I have to be authentic and find a way to communicate that but to do so in a way that will still be seen as helpful.

This dilemma often comes up when a client wants me to recommend or do a particular kind of "culture survey," or do something in a mindless way without considering the consequences. I could just say no, but that would not be helpful. To be helpful and consistent with this new model, I would prefer to say, "Tell me a little bit more about what you have in mind." "Why do you want to do this culture survey?" "What problem are you trying to solve?" And so on. To be able to do this requires adopting a new attitude in approaching those first contacts.

Humble Consulting Requires a New Attitude of Humility, a Commitment to Helping, and Curiosity

The essence of this new attitude is humility in the face of the complexity of the problems and humility in the relationship with the client in the sense that I am there to help work things out together, not to take over the problem and run with it. I am there to empathetically honor the difficulties that the client faces and to focus on him and the situation, not on my own needs to sell myself, my skills, and my insights.

This attitude can best be captured by saying that I am genuinely committed to helping and genuinely care for the client and his or her situation. To ensure that this gets through to the client from the beginning, I allow myself to become *genuinely curious*. It is honest, spontaneous curiosity that best conveys my interest and concern for the client. This attitude can thus be characterized best by three Cs—*commitment* to helping, *caring* for the client, and, above all, *curiosity*. I have found that this new attitude requires some new skills as well.

HC Requires New Listening and Responding Skills

The most important new skill is a different kind of listening. With all the books and programs on improving listening skills, I found that in doing this kind of consulting I had to learn yet another kind of listening than what is usually advocated, and that this new kind of listening was needed in order to know how to respond. I had to develop two kinds of empathy. Empathy One is to listen for and be curious about the actual situation or problem that the client is describing. Empathy Two is to listen for and be curious about what is really bothering the speaker as she is explaining the problem or the situation.

For example, a call comes in from a potential client who says, "I am concerned about the level of engagement of my employees. Could you help me build a culture of engagement?" Empathy One would be to explore what she means by "engagement" and "culture" by asking for examples. Empathy Two would be to ask, "What is it that is concerning you; why are you worried about this?"

We can listen for both things, but at some point we have to decide whether to pursue our curiosity about the content and the situation or our curiosity about the caller. In either case, we have to learn that we have a broad range of possible questions and reactions available to us, and it makes a difference which kinds of questions we choose to ask or which kinds of responses we choose to make. Similarly, we have a real choice in how much to personalize the situation by the kinds of questions we ask, or by the kinds of things we reveal about ourselves. An analysis of these initial choices will be the focus of Chapter 4.

Personalizing the relationship is common to all of these points and must therefore be looked at more closely in that it changes the fundamental role of the consultant/helper.

HC Is a New and Different "Personal Role" for the Consultant

The word *consulting* traditionally connotes "to help in the role of expert and/or doctor" by providing expert information, services, diagnoses, and prescriptions in the form of recommendations while, above all, keeping professional distance. Although this role may continue to work for well-defined technical problems, it has become less and less useful because "the problem" cannot be defined clearly enough to enable the helper to know what to do that would be really helpful.

In the new HC role, the consultant's primary purpose is to enable the client to figure out and make sense of what is really worrying her, what is really on her mind. The consultant has to become a *partner* and *helper* even in that first inquiry into what is going on and what is worrying the client. For example, in a video consultation with a group of leaders of five organizations that had recently merged, I was asked how the five groups might now get together to create a common marketing program so that the community would know what the new merged services were.

Instead of proposing something about team building for the five groups, I found myself asking questions about what the service actually was—literacy programs and remedial reading clinics—why they had merged, and what had gotten in the way of their developing a marketing program. In that process I gradually realized that what really worried them was not how to find common ground but that each group would lose its unique skill.

What we worked out together, even in this first phone call, was the adaptive move that they really had to make first. That adaptive move was to observe each other actually working and learn from this what was for each of the five groups their unique skill and how that might fit the community's needs. They did not need a common marketing program; they first needed to get to know one another at a more fundamental, personal level.

To elicit genuine information from the client and to be able to process it, the consultant must work together with the client at a more personal level, Level Two. How personalization plays out will be analyzed in greater detail in Chapter 5. To make this work the consultant must have the paradoxical ability to be empathetic to the client and to the client's situation yet not to be "content seduced" but to stay focused on various processes that are occurring between the consultant and the client. These various process choices will be the focus of Chapter 6.

Dealing with the new complex, messy problems will, in the end, require new and innovative responses from the consultant.

HC Encourages a Wider Range of Consultant Behavior Based on the Consultant Being Open, Authentic, and Innovative in the Relationship

What should be the basis of my action, of how I respond in dialogue with the client? Do I stick closely to just humble inquiry? Do I blurt out whatever is on my mind? Do I give advice when I think I know the answer? Do I reveal how the project may help me and how it fits into my skill set? Do I inquire based on needing to know how the client's issues connect to my skills, or do I just keep going with curiosity and see where it leads?

The answer may be "any of these," depending on the circumstances of the moment. If the goal is to build an open and trusting relationship, I have to try to be authentic. If I see something that does not make sense or asks something of me that I don't want to do, I have to say so and explain, knowing that in the explanation I may actually provide help by bringing up issues that the client may not have even thought of. As we will see in several cases, it was my unwillingness to do what the client wanted that led to real help.

Where is innovation in all of this? Aren't what I am calling adaptive moves just interventions with a new name? Some adaptive moves may indeed be the standard kinds of interventions if the conversation leads to that conclusion, but more often than not I have found that adaptive moves are usually shorter and often counterintuitive. If we change who is in the room, change who is doing the sense making, and also change the nature of the conversation from problem solving and discussion/debate to genuine *dialogue*, all kinds of new adaptive moves will occur to people, especially if we remember that a "move" is not necessarily part of any plan. It is just a move.

The new model for consultant behavior will be more like improvisation theater or a jazz band than formal scripts, rules, or standardized guides and checklists. A major part of this will be to change the nature of the conversation from discussion and/or debate into more of a dialogue around the campfire.

HC Will Be Most Effective If the New Conversations Become Dialogues

This element may be the most different from traditional models because a Level Two relationship makes it possible to have an entirely different kind of conversation, a dialogic joint exploration based on both consultant and client accepting the reality that neither of them knows where the conversation is going or what kinds of adaptive moves we may think of if we give up the typical goal-oriented competitive problem-solving discussion that we are so often pushed into by the pressures of time and our limited models of what a conversation could be. Getting the right people into the room and having a dialogic exploration of the complex mess may be the best model of the future of effective helping.

How the New Elements Fit Together Logically

As I reviewed my various cases over the years, I realized that the essence of this new model was already evident in many of my experiences, but I now have to pull it together and describe it for others. This new model does not tell me what to do, but it provides me a way to think about what is happening to clients and what attitudes and skills I have to develop to be really helpful to them. I call it *Humble* Consulting because I am in awe of the complexity of the problems and of the difficulties that clients face in trying to move forward.

I also realize that there is an intrinsic logic to this combination of new things that can best be viewed in terms of the following ten working propositions:

1. To be really helpful requires locating what the real problem is, that is, what is worrying the client?

2. To locate what is worrying the client requires open and trusting communication between client and helper.

3. To facilitate open and trusting communication requires building a Level Two personal working relationship that goes beyond the formal Level One professional relationship of most helping situations.

4. To build such a Level Two working relationship requires some amount of personalization of the relationship.

5. To personalize the relationship requires humble inquiry

by asking more-personal questions or revealing more-personal thoughts or feelings.

6. To build a personal Level Two relationship requires that the consultant convey this intention in the initial contact with the client.

7. To make sense of what is bothering the client, once a Level Two working relationship is building, helper and client must engage in a *joint* dialogic process.

8. To determine whether there are several things bothering the client for which no single solution will help requires careful review by both consultant and client.

9. To decide where action is needed, consultant and client have to *jointly decide* on priorities and what actions to take.

10. If the problem is simple and clear, the helper should go into the expert or doctor role or refer the client to an expert or doctor. If the problem turns out to be complex and messy, the client and helper should engage in a dialogue to figure out a feasible *adaptive move*, knowing that this may not *solve* the problem but will provide some comfort and will reveal new information on the basis of which to figure out the *next adaptive move*.

Adaptive moves have to be *joint decisions* because the consultant will never know enough about the client's personal situation or organizational culture, and the client will never know enough about all the consequences of a given intervention such as a survey or other diagnostic process tool. Therefore, one of the consultant's responsibilities is also to understand the consequences of certain kinds of adaptive moves such as diagnostic interviews and surveys, and to fully brief the client about those consequences to determine whether or not the client is ready for such moves.

What Does It Mean to Really Help?

I think of help as doing something with and for clients that they cannot do by themselves. The ultimate judgment of whether what I have done has been helpful or not is basically up to the client to decide. If I feel I have helped but the client has not felt helped, then I have not helped. So where does *really helping* fit by this criterion? In the kinds of complex, messy problems I have described, whether I am being helpful or not has to be perpetually evaluated by both the client and me. Sometimes the client will see things that have improved the situation or will have gained clarity about what to do next without my knowing it. Sometimes I will see things that have clearly improved the situation that the client has not perceived, and we will agree that help has been provided.

My clients and I will discover that the first real help is my enabling them to see the true complexity and messiness of the problem situation and help them to abandon quick fixes and/or knee-jerk reactions. Beyond that, the real help will be to evolve the right adaptive moves to deal with the realities of the situation that I help them to identify.

How Can HC Possibly Be Faster?

How HC can be faster is to some degree logical and to some degree paradoxical. Logically, it is faster because I am at the outset only trying to make enough sense of the complex mess to identify a next adaptive move, not an entire solution to an entire problem. It is paradoxical because that next move is often the real help. Once we humbly accept the reality of the problem's complexity and instability, we can give ourselves permission just to focus on what to do next and not worry about all the future next moves that might be down the road.

However, in order to be really helpful, that next move has to be culturally valid, so the exploration of what is culturally possible and/or desirable also has to be done faster. Having outsiders engage in a diagnostic process by gathering and analyzing data often turns out to be much slower than building a personal relationship with the client and other members of the system and together figuring out what is going on and what needs to be done. Where culture is involved, I have also learned that clients digging out what is their own culture (with my help) is not only faster but more valid and more likely to be accepted as reality by them. What is often most helpful is to make clients aware of the depth and complexity of the culture in which they live and to show them that simple culture diagnoses and "culture change fixes" rarely accomplish what the client wants.

Humble Consulting Will Be the New Leadership Skill

As the world of work becomes more complex, all leaders and managers will, from time to time, have to become helpers to their bosses, subordinates, and peers. Therefore, they too will have to discover that professional distance can be very destructive to teamwork. They too will have to learn how to build more-personal relationships, especially with their subordinates, in order to get the information they need to improve the quality and safety of the work to be done.

I have found it shocking how often communication across hierarchical and functional boundaries is faulty. Employees withhold information that is critical to safe performance or quality work, sometimes even lie, saying that things are okay when in fact they are not. Their managers would reassure me that they were good listeners and paid attention, but when their subordinates were interviewed, I would learn that they had tried to communicate upward and were met with indifference, impatience, and the killing dictum "don't bring me a problem if you don't have a solution."

I learned that managers felt that they had done their jobs when they had clearly *told* their subordinates what to do and how to do it. It seemed not to occur to them that they had to actually create a climate in which employees would feel welcomed if they admitted that they did not understand, or did not agree, or had bad news to report. When complex problems are identified, it is often the manager's job to work with the employee to figure out together what the problem and the approach to ameliorating it might be. Listening, even good empathetic listening, is not enough if the employee feels unsafe in bringing up a problem in the first place.

As work becomes more complex, bosses and subordinates may have to find ways to personalize their relationships with one another to facilitate more trust and open communication. This has clearly happened already in operating rooms and in other kinds of work groups that are highly interdependent. The big question for the future is—can leaders and managers learn to be humble consultants to their subordinates?

In conclusion, the messages of this book are directed primarily to consultants, coaches, and other kinds of helpers, but they are just as applicable to parents, bosses, and team members when they find themselves from time to time having to create a more personal helping relationship because they are dealing with a complex, messy problem.

THREE

The Need for a Trusting and Open Level Two Relationship

To fully understand how Humble Consulting (HC) is different requires a short journey into a bit of cultural analysis. We begin with what is a relationship in the first place, then identify four broad levels of relationship that are more or less identifiable in every society, and then home in on Level Two as the key to Humble Consulting.

What Is a Relationship? What Do We Mean by Trust and Openness?

We use the words *relationship*, *trust*, and *openness* glibly and frequently, as if we think that everyone will, of course, understand what we mean. Yet when we ask someone to define any one of these three words, we get either a blank stare, a disdainful look implying that we must be stupid, or definitions that don't really explain anything and that don't even agree with one another.

When we look these words up in the dictionary or in other works, we find equally vague terms like *connection*, *mutual dependence*, or *linkage*. The problem is that these terms are too abstract and can have many different meanings in different cultures and different situations. For purposes of understanding HC, we need to focus on what these terms mean in the situation where one person is trying to help another person on a complex problem in such a way that it will turn out to be really helpful.

A relationship is a set of *mutual expectations* about each other's future behavior based on past interactions with one another.

I have a relationship with you if I can more or less predict some of your behavior and you can more or less predict some of my behavior. In a shallow relationship, that might include just a vague sense of knowing what each of us will do; in a very deep relationship, each of us also knows how the other thinks, feels, and values things. In a shallow relationship, I can only trust you not to harm me and not to lie to me. In a good working relationship, I need to be able to predict how much I can count on you to make and keep your commitments and how open and reliable you will be in your communication with me. One could say that when we have a "good relationship," this means that we feel a certain level of comfort with the other person, comfort that is based on this sense of each of us knowing how the other will react and that we are both working toward a goal that we have agreed upon. That feeling of comfort is often what we mean by the word *trust*.

Relationship is an *interactive* concept and must therefore be analyzed from a sociological point of view of interactions. It is not enough for one party to say "I feel I have a connection (relationship) with you" if the other party does not feel that connection. Unrequited love is not a relationship, but a casual friendship can be a relationship. If I trust my boss but he does not trust me, there is no relationship. If I am quite open with my boss but he is not open with me, there is no relationship.

For a relationship to work, there must be some symmetry

in mutual expectations, a symmetry that is worked out over time with a series of interactions that serve as a kind of test of how deep the relationship is to be. I cannot determine how much to trust you and how open to expect you to be with me if we have not had a series of interactions where our observations of each other served as little tests in the process of building the relationship.

When we say that a relationship can be casual or deep, we are acknowledging the key insight that relationships exist on a dimension where at one extreme we have minimal predictability and virtually no emotional involvement, and at the other extreme we have very intense emotional involvement and can predict quite a lot about each other. This point is critical because when we get to the issue of how to build a relationship, we have to recognize that it is ultimately a *joint* responsibility and that the building process is a series of interactions where each party is implicitly measuring the depth of the relationship after each interaction.

The depth of a relationship is a *mutual decision* based on the comfort level that each party arrives at through interaction. We all are quite sensitive to when a relationship is "going too far," or when it is "failing" because one or the other person is "not willing to go farther" or has done something unexpected and unacceptable. If we are trying to define how to be *really helpful* to each other, it becomes useful to consider what level of trust and openness will be required in the relationship.

Culturally Defined Levels of Relationship, Trust, and Openness

All societies have ways of stratifying their citizens in terms of rank, status, and expected degree of connectedness. Table 1

TABLE 1. Levels of Trust and Openness in Relationships

Level Minus One: Negative hostile relationship, exploitation

Examples: Prisoners, POWs, slaves, members of different cultures, elderly or emotionally ill people, the victims or marks for criminals or con men

Level One: Acknowledgment, civility, transactional and professional role relations

Examples: Strangers on the street, seatmates on trains and planes, service people whose help we need, professional helpers such as doctors and lawyers

Comment: We do not know one another as individuals but treat one another as fellow humans whom we trust to a certain degree not to harm us and with whom we have polite levels of openness in conversation. Professional helpers such as doctors and lawyers fall into this category because their role definition requires them to maintain a "professional distance."

Level Two: Recognition as a unique person

Examples: People whom we know as individuals, co-workers, clients, bosses or subordinates whom we have gotten to know personally but not intimately through common work or educational experiences, casual friendships

Comment: This kind of relationship implies a deeper level of trust and openness in terms of (1) making and honoring commitments and promises to each other, (2) agreeing not to undermine each other or harm what we are endeavoring to do, and (3) agreeing not to lie to each other or withhold information relevant to our task.

Level Three: Close friendships, love, and intimacy

Examples: Relationships with strong positive emotions

Comment: *Intimacy implies more openness and not only no harm but active support whenever needed.* This kind of relationship is usually viewed as undesirable in work or in helping situations.

shows the levels of relationship from which we can build the Level Two working relationship concept that is necessary for HC.

Minus One: Negative Relationships

This level pertains only to the unusual situation where we basically do not treat one another as human at all, as might be the case between a slave master and slaves, a prison guard and prisoners, or, sadly, some caretakers of emotionally sick or elderly patients of a hospital or nursing home. In the organizational world, we would rarely expect to find such exploitation or indifference, but we occasionally discover it in sweatshops, in the factories of some other countries, and, unfortunately, in the attitudes of some managers who view their employees as merely hired hands, leading some employees to characterize their work situation as "inhuman."

Level One: Transactional, Bureaucratic, and Professional Relationships

This large category is very much taken for granted by all of us as our normal relationship to strangers. What we don't realize is that the psychological and social distance that we experience with strangers actually includes a considerable degree of openness and trust, based on the cultural rules of civility, good manners, tact, and political correctness that make commercial activities viable. We expect a great deal of one another in our various transactional relations when we have needs of services of various kinds, when we engage in the bureaucratic relationships of organizational life, and, most relevant to this analysis, in the role-related relations that we call "professional."

As members of civilized society, we expect, at the minimum, to *acknowledge* one another as fellow humans. We
expect others to notice our presence even if we don't know
each other. Level One relationships are expected to be imper-
sonal and relatively free of emotion. They are highly routin-
ized exchanges of give and take based on mutual expectations. I give you something, you say thank you; you ask me a
question, I feel obligated to answer. This is so automatic that
we notice it only when it breaks down, when someone is not
civil, or when someone gets "too personal."

Much helping behavior falls into this Level One, such as
when we require the help of various service people to build,
maintain, and fix things, when we need the help of salespeople, and when we ask strangers for directions or for help
with some chore. In all of these situations, we exhibit what
I will call *Level One trust* in that we expect civil behavior,
we expect not to be taken advantage of, and we expect to
be helped. We also assume *Level One openness* in that we
expect accurate and helpful communication relevant to the
request. We learn that these expectations and their associated "rules" of behavior apply situationally and according to
the various roles we engage in. Are we just asking someone
for directions, or are we requesting some specific service, as
when we deal with a maintenance person, salesperson, or
clerk? Level One role relations get complicated when we deal
with so-called professional helpers—doctors, lawyers, min-
isters, and official human relations helpers such as social
workers, counselors, and psychiatrists.

PROFESSIONAL DISTANCE AND THE ASYMMETRY
OF PROFESSIONAL RELATIONSHIPS

One of the main problems in day-to-day interactions with
professionals is that they enjoy a special status associated

with their education, knowledge, skill, and licenses to perform special helping services. With that status goes the privilege that they can be as personal as their helping role requires, but the relationship is not symmetric. You cannot ask your doctors the same personal questions as they can ask you. Furthermore, they must act as if even the most personal things you reveal about your situation must be treated impersonally, as just information relative to the diagnosis and treatment, not as personal details about you.

This impersonality is strongly reinforced by the extensive societal rules about privacy. Even if the female patient reveals to her therapist that she is attracted to him, professionalism clearly prohibits the therapist from taking advantage of that information and getting into a more intimate relationship with her. The professional helper is bound by the norms and rules of that profession and would normally limit his inquiry to information relevant to the area of help. The urologist or dermatologist might get very personal about your recent sexual activity, but the orthopedic surgeon or dentist would normally not feel licensed to ask about it. All of this can be really helpful when the problem to be addressed is technical. However, these Level One relationships break down when the consulting help involves complex organizational problems of the type I have described.

WHEN LEVEL ONE HELP IS OR IS NOT HELPFUL

Level One professional relationships work only to the extent that the helper has correctly diagnosed the problem and has solutions available that will work. That, in turn, depends on whether the client has correctly identified the problem, has clearly conveyed what the problem is, and has chosen a helper who can work on that problem. What I have observed over and over again is that the client may feel at a disadvantage for having had to ask for help in the first place, and is therefore not too trusting and open with you at the outset, and is not likely to be highly motivated to reveal what is really on his mind. He has no particular reason to trust you until the two of you have interacted and he has calibrated how you have reacted to his initial request. He may not even be aware of what is really on his mind while he is busy testing the relationship to see whether it is safe to get more personal (Schein, 2009).

The client asking you for help may even unwittingly "content seduce" you into your official area of expertise and thereby get you preoccupied with your own personal skills and agenda. You may feel flattered, you will be relieved that someone wants to employ you, you will perhaps see some much-needed income ahead, you will be thinking about how much time or energy you have for this, you will wonder whether you will have to travel and where this call is coming from. But in all of this preoccupation with yourself and your role as helper, you probably will miss two other important thoughts and feelings: does this request elicit a feeling of caring about the person, and does this arouse your curiosity, either about the person or about the issue presented?

If you jump in too fast with how you believe you can help, there is always the danger that you will begin to work on the wrong problem because you have not explored enough what is going on. You cannot assume that the client will be sufficiently trusting and open for you to get accurate diagnostic information on what the client's problem really is and what the client will actually do with what you might recommend. We know that even in regular medicine, patients withhold information because they are rushed in the diagnostic interview and don't tell the doctor where it really hurts, that they are too nervous to reveal some things, that they can't really take the particular pills that were prescribed or follow a particular therapeutic routine. They may even lie that they have done what the doctor recommended because they don't trust the doctor to be sympathetic to their noncompliance.

Because Level One professional relationships encourage impersonality and politeness, the patient would not be expected to say "Look, doctor, I feel rushed, you are not looking at me, so I don't feel able to tell you all I know about my condition." Instead, the patient would most likely feel that "I don't like being rushed, I did forget to tell the doctor a few things that I remembered later at home, but she seemed to get all the information she needed, so I will trust her to know what she is doing." Unfortunately, wrong diagnoses and prescriptions that do harm do occur. Clients collude in this pathological process when they feel that they also have to be brief and efficient because they are being charged by the hour or because they attribute extraordinary diagnostic skills to the doctor.

Unfortunately, much of organizational and management consulting operates by these Level One norms and procedures. The consultant comes in, accepts the assignment on the basis of what the client initially presents, uses all kinds of tools to do a formal diagnosis, and presents formal recommendations. These procedures often get the client so dependent on the consultant's diagnostic processes that the real underlying problem never surfaces. It is then too late for the client to say out loud, "This is very interesting but not exactly what I had in mind. I learned a lot, but I don't see how I can really use what you have recommended." This is Level One pseudohelp that does not provide *real* help for complex problems. So what is Level Two?

Level Two Personal Relationships

The essence of Level Two is that the client moves from being a "case," a stranger who must be kept professionally distant, to being a unique person with whom you can have a more personal relationship. The essence of HC is that the helper begins to build that relationship from the first contact by opening the door to *personalization,* by which I mean that both the client and the consultant begin to treat each other as persons rather than roles.

The consultant does not engage in Level One scouting, diagnosing, and analyzing but immediately shows curiosity about and interest in the client and the client's situation because the goal is to find out as quickly as possible what is really on the client's mind. The consultant works to build that personal relationship from the beginning to increase the chances to identify a *workable* problem and to avoid going into a useless or harmful set of diagnostic processes and interventions. I see useless and dangerous diagnostic processes happen all the time, especially with culture creation and culture change programs.

A manager calls a consultant to "create a culture of teamwork," or "engagement," or "customer service," and the consultant offers a program. Neither one realizes that you cannot "create" culture unless you are the founder of a new group and impose your values on it. Even then it does not become a culture unless the group is successful and those founder values come to be taken for granted. Time and money are spent on the diagnostic surveys, but unless the consultant finds out what the manager is really worried about, little useful help will have been provided.

Getting personal in this context means that the consultant creates a conversation in which it is more likely to come out just what is bothering the client, what she really wants to accomplish, and what kinds of things might be possible to do in the existing culture. The humble consultant does not open the door to *anything* personal but tries to create a climate where the client might become trusting enough to reveal what is really bothering her and what kind of help she really needs.

Of course, Level Two is a remarkably broad category that covers everything from the more personalized helping that I am advocating here to various kinds of friendships or even personal acquaintanceship with our Level One transactional helpers. We get to know a repairman or a salesman when we discover some common interest or past history and add to the formal relationship a Level Two personal element. The dilemma in defining such a relationship in the helping context is that the personalization I am advocating has to occur around the mutual goal of helping and being really helped. What I learn about a stranger on a long airplane ride or when we share a long fire drill is personal, but it may not be relevant to a joint effort to solve that stranger's problems, should he become a client. The Level Two relationship has to be built around the joint task that the helper and client are engaged in. It is bounded by the cultural rules that apply to situations of giving and receiving help. Those situational rules help to define what we mean by "trust" and "openness" in the helping context.

Trust and openness in Level Two. We do trust strangers up to a point. So what is so different about Level Two's trust and openness? There is nothing in a Level One relationship that guarantees enough openness that you can count on others to tell you the truth as it pertains to the task and, most important, to volunteer information that may influence how well or safely the task is being accomplished. There is nothing in a Level One relationship that guarantees that others will make promises and/or commitments, and keep them. If we are engaging in a helping relationship, we need to achieve a level in which both the helper and the client tell the truth, volunteer information, make commitments and promises, and honor those commitments and promises.

In a Level Two relationship, the helper is authentic and expresses her doubts about a particular diagnostic process or intervention that the client proposes and is willing to pay for, and she would count on the client to express his doubts about where the helping process was leading if he had such doubts. In a Level Two relationship, the helper would ask sincerely from time to time, "Is what we are doing really helping?" and she would expect the client to give an honest answer.

Task- and goal-related personalization. As the cases in this book show, when either the client or the helper chooses to personalize, the personalization is usually constrained by the initial assumption that both are there to create a helping relationship. If a client calls me and asks if I would do a culture survey for him, a Level One response might be "Sure, what do you have in mind?" indicating a readiness to provide him the expert service he is asking for. If I am operating as a humble consultant and trying to personalize the relationship toward Level Two, I might say, "Tell me more," or "Why do you want to do a culture survey?" or "What do you have in mind?" or "What do you mean by culture?" or "Why did you decide to call me?"

Alternatively, I can try to personalize by revealing something more personal about myself. I could say, "In my experience I have found such surveys work only if they are linked to a clear business problem." Such questions or revelations both invite and subtly force the client into a more personal conversation and will often move us to what is really on the client's mind more rapidly.

Notice, however, that such questions are relevant to the situation that the client opens with. It would not occur to me at that point to ask "How old are you?" or "What is your family situation," which might be appropriate in another context such as on a blind date. The personalization has to occur around the basic tacit assumption that this is a meeting of one person seeking some kind of help and another person trying to be helpful. How this plays out as the relationship evolves will be discussed in the later chapters, but for now I want to be clear that the decision to personalize into a Level Two relationship is designed to build trust and the consequent openness to find out what is really on the client's mind within the cultural context of the helping situation.

If the client accepts the invitation and responds in a personal way, the relationship enters that testing phase where, with each interaction, we continue to choose whether to get more or less personal as the situation affords. But it is important to realize that the conversation remains task related. We don't become instant friends, because that is not our purpose, but we may become highly open and frank around why we actually think that a particular survey might or might not be helpful. I know of one example where the client wanted a particular kind of intervention that I kept challenging. After an extended conversation in which trust was building up, the client finally revealed that she had been asked to do it by a board member and had promised to do it even though she had doubts herself. Her real problem turned out to be that she did not know how to deal with this board member, so we switched into a useful coaching session on that issue.

Content versus process. Another important issue to consider is whether we personalize around the presenting problem or around the manner in which the client is presenting it and the process that the client is proposing. I can get extremely curious about the content of what the client has presented to me or around the process that the client is proposing. The client may say, "I have an engagement problem in my organization and would therefore like to do a culture survey." I have several choices of how to respond, that is, what to become curious about. For example, I might ask (1) "What do you mean by the word *engagement*?" or (2) "What is worrying you about lack of engagement?" or (3) "Why do you want to do a survey?" or (4) "Why did you choose to call me at this time? What is going on?"

I would be probing three different kinds of processes: the client's thought and problem-solving process, the client's clarity of thought about how to proceed, and the client's assumptions about what the consultant should do. I may agree to doing a survey but want to steer him to an organization that would combine the individualized survey with group interviews if he really wants to get at the nature of the culture. This response invites the client to explore why I might want the group interviews and leads ultimately to a better joint decision of what the next move might be. The point is that the ultimate joint decision on which process to use will be valid only if we have established enough of a Level Two relationship to elicit from both of us what we really think.

To summarize, with complex, nontechnical, messy problems, a Level Two task-oriented relationship becomes necessary in order to create enough trust that the real motives, issues, and concerns of both helper and client surface. This level of personalization remains task focused and is only as deep as needed. It does not imply emotional attachments or personal information that might be regarded as intimate in the society. In fact, we usually accept the reality that getting intimate with a client is not desirable. But as helpers we have to learn that while Level Three is going too far, Level One is not enough. We have to learn to personalize to an optimal Level Two.

Level Three: Intimacy and Emotional Attachment, Friendship and Love

Level Three relationships are what we might call "intimate" or "close," friendships that go beyond the more casual connections that can occur in Level Two. This level is more emotionally charged and implies all of the trust and openness of Level Two, but, in addition, it assumes that we will actively support each other as needed and actively display emotional, loving behavior toward each other.

We want to avoid Level Three in organizational work because it can cause fraternization, nepotism, and/or degrees of favoritism that are considered to be an impediment to getting work done and are often labeled in our culture as "corrupt" when they occur in the business or work arena. Therapists are not supposed to get involved in the personal lives of their patients. Office romances are considered inappropriate. Gifts and payoffs are considered illegitimate as incentives to get things done. These and other norms of appropriate and inappropriate personalization apply to all helping relationships as well.

If we are talking about a Level Three intimate relationship or friendship, the cultural rules of what one should be open about expand in that we deepen our relationship through successive cycles of revealing more and more of our private feelings, reactions, and observations, and we calibrate the level of acceptance by the other person of what we are revealing by their reciprocation of more revelations of his or her own. We ask more-personal intimate questions of each other and test whether they are well received or offensive and thereby learn what level of intimacy feels comfortable.

Even intimate relationships have clear boundaries and vary in how deep they get. What we have learned in our culture when we grew up provides guidelines and limits for such openness, and we all build up our own sense of what we consider private, to be shared only with exceptionally intimate friends and family members. Occasionally, we will find tasks and situations such as Navy Seals or Army Rangers doing an operation together that require some level of intimate knowledge of how each person works, because accomplishing the task itself requires a high degree of collaboration.

In defining these levels, I am not asserting that the boundaries are initially clear or that the responses of others are always predictable. Part of building the Level Two relationship is to mutually discover the boundaries of personalization as each party calibrates how the other responds to a change in level of openness and finds that level of comfort where we feel we trust each other and can count on each other to be open and truthful.

Summary of the Levels

I have discussed four levels of relationship marked by different degrees of trust and openness. These definitions of the four levels are fairly clear at the extremes, but when we are defining "helping relationships," we have to acknowledge that within Level Two there is still a broad range of possibilities of what we mean by trust and openness. The humble consultant must build a Level Two relationship by becoming more personal, either in what she asks or in what she reveals, but she must, at the same time, avoid the formality of Level One professional distance or the violation of privacy that would be felt with Level Three intimate questions or revelations. A great part of the skill of the helper is in managing this balance between being too formal at one extreme and too intimate at the other extreme.

Though the boundaries between these levels may be quite fuzzy, the principle is that Humble Consulting requires a Level Two relationship. Professional Level One relationships do not solve or ameliorate complex human problems, and Level Three relationships are considered ethically out of bounds in virtually all modern professional contexts. If the Level Two joint exploration of what is really the problem reveals that there is a technical solution, a fix that can be implemented, the humble consultant would either have the skills herself and apply them or would help the client find the right expert consultant or doctor to provide the solution. If the problem remains ill defined, complex, messy, and constantly changing, then the role of the humble consultant is to continue to help the client define and implement adaptive moves that will improve the situation.

Case Illustrations

My own insight into what is involved in HC grew over a number of years of experience. It is especially in cases where the boundaries of the relationship were ignored that I developed some of the insights on the consequences of operating at different levels.

CASE 2. Good Intentions, Not Much Help: The Engineering Interviews

I present this case because it fits the traditional consulting Level One model and illustrates how that model can utterly fail to be helpful while wasting valuable organizational and helping resources. Early in my assistant professorship at the MIT Sloan School, my mentor and boss, Doug McGregor, asked a colleague and me, "Would you like to help a neighboring company to improve its engineering operations by interviewing the engineers to find out what is and is not working, then summarize your findings and present them to the head of Engineering?" Doug explained that the request had come to him from the VP of Administration, and the process was set up for us by the company. In effect, we were being hired as organizational "doctors" to examine this group as a patient, to make a diagnosis, and to recommend solutions. And we would be paid to do this. It was my first introduction to the world of management consulting.

The administrative secretary of the Engineering Department set up rooms, established an interview schedule, and told the engineers by means of a memo that we would be talking to them. We completed the interviews over a period of a month or so; carefully analyzed all the data; and prepared a report that highlighted things that were working, things that needed improvement, and comments about management. At the end we made several recommendations that reflected our best diagnosis of what was wrong and how to fix it.

We set up a two-hour interview with the head of Engineering, gave him the report, and were prepared to explain how he could improve his department. He looked at the table of contents, found the section on management, read some of the comments that were clearly critical of his management style, became somewhat stone-faced, thanked us very much, and terminated the meeting.

We never heard from him or anyone else in the company again, so we never learned whether we had helped or harmed or been irrelevant. We had done our job, so we also did not discuss the whole process with McGregor. We did, however, have a strong sense that this had "failed" in some way.

LESSONS: WHERE HAD OUR CONSULTING MODEL "FAILED"?

■ From my perspective now, we failed in almost every possible way. We never spoke to the VP of Administration or the head of Engineering before launching the interviews, so we had no idea what their goals or possible hidden agendas might have been. They were Level One strangers to us at the beginning and throughout the project. Even more to the point, we never discussed with the head of Engineering what we would ask about, or alerted him to the reality that his management style would be in the report. We should not have been surprised that our feedback meeting with him was stiff, formal, and unproductive.

■ We went into the interviews with no sense of who the client really was, what problems were being solved, or even what "improving" meant. We were arrogant enough to believe that we knew what "improvement" meant in some absolute sense. We did not explore with Doug McGregor what he had in mind in offering us this assignment.

- We had focused entirely on being good "scientists," doing a thorough diagnosis through competent interviews; a careful content analysis; and a complete summary of what worked, what didn't, and what we thought should be done differently. As scientists "gathering data," we never considered what issues were on the mind of management or what change goals they had. Was the Engineering Department not productive or innovative enough? Was there a morale problem or too much turnover? We never knew how the project connected to the business problems the organization was trying to address. All this was scientifically irrelevant to the role we had accepted.

- We had the illusion that our careful diagnosis and recommendations spoke for themselves! I learned for the first time that diagnosing a system just for the sake of diagnosis is not very helpful because in any complex system one can diagnose it from multiple points of view, just as a personality can be diagnosed from many points of view. Diagnosing organizations and/or cultures for their own sake is not helpful. It may be scientifically "interesting," but if we are trying to help, it works better if there is some problem or issue that is driving the need for a diagnosis.

- In summary, the biggest lesson was that being a scientist gathering data is not the same thing as being a helper. Even when a particular diagnostic tool touts scientific reliability and validity, which may be helpful to the scientist trying to "measure" the organization for some research purposes, it is not necessarily helpful to the client trying to solve a problem. This insight was strongly reinforced some years later when I did a scientific group analysis of the culture of an organization as part of an executive development program. I thought it was fascinating. The group thought it was boring and wondered why we were doing it. For them it did not connect to anything. For me it was research data. The two things are not the same.

CASE 3. Adventures with Digital Equipment Corporation

My relationship with Digital Equipment Corporation (DEC) began in the mid-1960s and continued into the mid-1990s. My many helping adventures with DEC provided an enormous amount of learning throughout these years and culminated in a book about the growth and death of this organization (Schein, 2003). My early interventions provided me, without my realizing it at the time, crucial learning opportunities that led to the concept of *process consultation* and laid the foundations for Humble Consulting.

THE INITIAL MEETING AND THE PROPOSITION

My relationship with DEC resulted from having a Level Two relationship with Win Hindle, whom I had gotten to know when he was in the Industrial Liaison Office at MIT in the late 1950s. He was recruited by Ken Olsen, DEC's co-founder, to be Ken's executive assistant, and, in that capacity, he called me one day to find out if I was interested in doing some work with DEC. I said I was, which resulted in a meeting with Ken "to test our chemistries." When I went to meet him at his office, I found a decidedly informal man, surrounded by computer memorabilia and outdoor gear. He seemed to want to discuss mostly his canoeing and various other outdoor activities and managed to convey to me that the reason he was willing to have me come in as a consultant was very much related to his general faith in MIT and its faculty.

His proposition was that I attend the regular Friday afternoon Operations Committee meetings "to see if I could help with communications and making the group work well." He did not say that there were any problems but explained, "We are a bunch of engineers, so it might be useful to have a social psychologist around to help us. You should just attend and see if you can help." I had very little opportunity to say anything or to ask questions in this opening exploration because Ken seemed to have it all figured out and made it clear that he did not expect any comments from me. He told me that his secretary would give me the details of time and location, and dismissed me.

At this point we were still in a Level One relationship, and I had no idea what I would find and where it would lead. What a gift to a young professor/consultant to be asked to "just observe and see if you can help." The headquarters in Maynard, Massachusetts, was just a half hour away from Cambridge, which made attending the Friday meetings extremely easy.

My confidence in accepting this assignment was fed by my having had several summers of experience as a staff member in the Human Relations Labs that were conducted each summer at Bethel, Maine. These labs were built around Kurt Lewin's theories, and they launched in the 1950s what has come to be taken for granted as "experiential education." The key learning took place in the T-groups (training groups), where participants and staff members together created an environment for learning about groups and leadership (Schein and Bennis, 1965).

EARLY GROUP INTERVENTION

From my Bethel experience, I thought I knew what a good group should look like and, unconsciously, was still locked into my role as a scientist who could analyze, make suggestions, and thereby "improve things." Ken introduced me to the group with the same broad mandate and said I would mostly just observe to see how the group worked and try to be helpful. I think I was accepted by the group to some degree at Level One because Ken was, in effect, vouching for me. Taking on the mantle of the "group doctor" and launching into listening politely to learn as much as I could from observing the group's behavior became easy and natural.

I noticed after one or two meetings, in which I said nothing, that the group worked from a written agenda that they did not finish and that they were frustrated not to finish because important items had not been discussed before time ran out. At the third meeting, I saw the same tension building up, so I decided to ask a humble inquiry question.

Ed S.: *Excuse me, could I ask a question? Where did this agenda come from?*

(Group members looked at each other with puzzled expressions.)

Ken: *I have my administrative secretary prepare it . . .*

(More confused looks.)

Ken: *Let's bring her in, and let's find out how she prepares it.*

(Ken's assistant is brought in.)

Ken: *Hi, Marge, we were wondering how you prepare our weekly agenda . . .*

Marge: *Well, it is just the items that each of you on the Operations Committee tell me that you need to discuss this week. I put them down in the order in which they are called in, and you get that list as your agenda. Is that okay? Do you want me to do something different?*

(Nobody spoke up immediately, but there was an aura in the room of recognizing that this way of creating the agenda made no sense. Ken then took charge.)

Ken: *No, Marge, that is perfectly fine; continue to do it that way, thanks . . .*

(When Marge was gone, Ken continued.)

Ken: *We obviously have items of different urgency, so starting next week when we first get the list from Marge, let's take five minutes and identify the firefighting items that must be done.*

(There was a lot of head nodding and a sigh of satisfaction and relief that they might in future meetings feel less frustrated. Needless to say, I was extremely proud of having helped the group with my innocent ignorance, but I did not appreciate until many years later that this was a perfect case of "process help," that is, using one's ignorance strategically and tactically by identifying an issue that may or may not be a problem and timing the question carefully to a moment when the group can observe the phenomenon for itself and make its own judgment about what to do differently.)

A week or two passed, and the group did get through a lot of their firefighting items, but important policy questions now kept getting shoved further and further into the future, leading me to wonder how they might ever get to some of those big questions. I decided to raise the issue as a provocative question, a thoroughly different kind of intervention.

Ed S.: *I notice that some of the important policy items keep getting delayed. Should you have more than one kind of meeting where at some meetings you take up the policy questions first?*

> (This was a jump to a more suggestive inquiry, which seemed appropriate since the group was exceptionally efficiency oriented and could hear what amounted to a new process suggestion.)

Group member: *Why don't we start doing that on alternate Fridays?*

> (I had observed that the group got tired at their Friday afternoon meetings, so I wondered to myself if I should bring that up as a reason not to have them just alternate Fridays. I had to choose whether to stay in the inquiry mode or shift to some other form of question or even make a direct suggestion because I really wanted to challenge their proposed solution. I experienced this moment as shifting further into the doctor role, where I was about to make a diagnosis and maybe even a prescription. This seemed justified to me because when it came to running effective meetings, I thought I was more of an expert than the group was.)

Ed S.: *For your policy meetings, would it not be better to have a longer meeting?*

Group member: *I agree, so we should start the Friday meetings earlier.*

(This did not seem to me to solve the problem, and I had begun to think about the possibility that they would get deeper into their issues if they met away from the office.)

Ed S.: *Do you really want to discuss important policy issues here at the office on a Friday afternoon?*

(This comment was more provocation and authentically revealed some of my impatience with their failure to see how dysfunctional it would be to spend tired Friday afternoons on important matters.)

Group member: *No, you're right, Ed. Let's meet away from the office to talk about the important product and production decisions when we are less tired.*

Ken: *Why don't we go up to my cabin in the Maine woods for a weekend . . .*

(I sensed an immediate positive response to this idea and watched with interest how other group members picked it up, offered cabins of their own, and went into an intense problem-solving mode. They decided within a few minutes to have periodic all-day meetings away from the office at one of their cabins in the woods. These meetings eventually migrated into quarterly whole-weekend retreats where most of the important strategic decisions were made, thus permitting the Friday meetings to become more focused on immediate problems that could be addressed in that format. The quarterly retreats were called "Woods Meetings" and became a regular part of DEC's governance structure throughout its history.)

LESSONS

■ I had learned from the earlier intervention around the agenda that the group could solve its own problem quickly once a problem was clearly identified. I was therefore not surprised that once the idea of important meetings away from the office was launched, the group would quickly invent a whole new process that I would not have thought of but that clearly fitted well into their New England outdoor, woodsy culture.

■ I had seen in this process how culture is created. A group creates a new process and new structure to solve a particular problem, and if the solution works, it becomes routine and the group forgets when and where the idea came from. Years later, people took Woods Meetings for granted as the way to solve the big problems. The head of Engineering, who was a member of the Operations Committee, liked the idea so much that he instituted such meetings for his engineering heads and called them "Jungle Meetings."

■ I had remembered from the days of facilitating sensitivity training groups how important it was to time interventions carefully to moments when the client group had enough information to be able to see the problem for themselves. The intervention then is just a nudge and a kind of permission to innovate. I also noticed that one could get a lot accomplished with diagnostic questions that did not force new ideas into the client's thinking but put the ideas out there for the client to grab if the idea made sense.

■ The most important lesson was that I could switch roles from just asking humble inquiry questions to being the expert who knew that long Friday afternoon meetings would not lead to effective policy and strategy discussions. Once I knew that I had expert knowledge based on my own group experience, it was entirely appropriate and authentic to share that knowledge with the group in the form of a suggestive question on process.

■ I also noticed that with each intervention of this sort that helped the group have better meetings, my credibility increased and people stopped me in the hall to chat, leading to my really getting to know each of them individually. We were now all working toward Level Two relationships that later became crucial as problem complexity increased. As I look back on these times, I was edging toward the complex role I am now describing as **Humble Consulting**. In retrospect most of these interventions were what I am now calling **adaptive moves**.

■ Finally, I learned from these early experiences with the DEC group that being around an organization while it is doing real work surfaces real problems rapidly. Ken was an intuitive leader who sensed that he did not have to specify for me what problems to look for but, instead, just had to invite me into the organization to observe and draw my own conclusions about when and how to help. This sometimes worked beautifully, as I describe later, and sometimes was difficult, as I describe next.

TRYING TO FIX THE UNRULY GROUP

When the Woods Meetings became a regular event, I was typically invited to attend them. At one of the early ones, I observed a more extreme version of what I had seen on the Friday afternoons—constant interruptions of one another's points, high emotions, verbal put-downs, and generally unruly behavior that included people reading their e-mails, wandering off to sit in another part of the room, and in other ways actively showing disinterest in what was being discussed. Ken himself would wander off into a corner and stack Coke cans or in other ways play around, but of course he was listening intently and would suddenly enter the conversation with great intensity and a raised voice.

When I saw that this was a pattern, I decided to intervene. I observed one member trying to make a point and being rudely interrupted by another member.

Ed S.: *Could I just take a minute to point something out that might be helpful? Jack was trying to make a point, but before he was through, Pete interrupted him to make his own point. That seemed to cut off some information, and I wondered whether you noticed that this happens frequently in the group.*

Jack (smiling): *Yeah, I didn't get to say what I wanted.*

Pete: *Ed, you are right. Sorry Jack, just felt I had to make my point, but I agree that we should not cut each other off and interrupt so much. Thanks, Ed, for pointing this out.*

My satisfaction with this intervention was short-lived as, in subsequent conversations, it was as if I had never said anything. The interruptions, the emotional behavior, and the other unruly things continued as before. I remember trying a couple of more times to point those things out, being thanked each time for being "very helpful," and producing no change at all.

LESSONS

- The main lesson was learned much later: I had been the punishing expert telling the group that it was doing something bad. I had even violated one of the rules I had learned in sensitivity group facilitation of **observing** behavior but **not judging** it. Let the group judge it or consider what the consequences were of interrupting one another. By saying that I saw this often in the group, I was clearly implying that this was undesirable behavior. They were a bad group. In retrospect this intervention violated most of the principles I had learned about how to help a group learn.

- As I reflect on this from the point of view of HC, I realize that I was listening for how the group's behavior did or did not match **my ideal model** and had totally suppressed my curiosity about **why** the group behaved the way it did. I had failed one of my principles, that of "access your ignorance," which means to focus on what you **don't know,** in this case why the group was so unruly and emotional.

- The big point is that I was still being the doctor and scientist, still working from my own model of what is a "good group process," and not paying enough attention to what was really going on. I had forgotten that smart people don't do stupid things for no reason, so one must locate why they are doing something that looks stupid from our point of view but may make sense from their point of view. I learned that groups will do what they will do and remembered that the good-group model I had learned in the Human Relations Labs was designed to facilitate **learning.** Maybe this group had a different goal for which a different process was required, or possibly this unruly process solved problems for them in some way that I did not yet understand.

MY BREAKTHROUGH INTERVENTION

When the unruly behavior continued, I gave up trying to change them and lapsed into just sitting back and watching. In retrospect that was the moment when I became potentially really helpful because I abandoned my preoccupation with myself and my models of "good group behavior." I became caring and curious, key elements of the HC attitude. I had come to like these people, begun to feel sorry for them when they cut one another off and were rude, but, most important, begun to empathize with what they were trying to do. I began to listen to them instead of trying to figure out how to fix them. I will come back to this point later because in all of the advice on how to listen better, I feel we have not differentiated enough the choices we have on *what to listen for.* I decided to listen for "what are they trying to do anyway?"

Listening for what they were trying to do made several things clear: They were an extremely young company with some success under their belt, now trying to figure out what new products they should design and sell to keep growing. They were one of the very first companies to create *interactive computing,* a whole new concept that would ultimately make desktop personal computing routine, but no one at this point had the answer of just how to move forward. They were inventing the future, and each product decision was, in fact, betting the company. No wonder they were intense and emotional and each fighting for his or her own solution for what to do next and how to do it. They had been hired to be the best and the brightest and the most passionate.

I also noticed that I had trouble tracking the various alternatives that were being proposed and debated, so one day, quite without knowing what was motivating me except my *curiosity* to track things better, I went to the flipchart, and the following scene took place.

Jack: *Here is my idea, we take this line of computers and . . .*

Pete (interrupting): *Jack, you just don't understand, we have to . . .*

(I am now standing at the flipchart with marker in hand, looking directly at Jack, and interrupting Pete.)

Ed S.: *Jack, I started to write down your idea but didn't get all of it. What were you proposing?*

Jack: *Yeah, what I was trying to say is . . .*

(He then continues with the entire idea while Pete and the whole group listen and I write the idea down.)

Pete: *I see what you were saying. Now my point was . . .*

(I start to write it down, and the group listens for all of Pete's point until it is written down. The group then goes on but lets me write each major point down and continues in this more disciplined process until the major ideas are on the flipchart. The group now talks in terms of which idea they are agreeing with, critiquing, shooting down, or whatever, but the flipchart focuses the discussion toward some kind of consensus.)

At the end of that meeting, various group members come up to me and say, "Ed, what you did today, that was really helpful."

LESSONS

- The experience I have recounted above is probably the most important learning experience of my whole consulting career because it showed me the power of giving up my own model, learning to listen to what the client group was trying to do, and then doing something that helped them do what **they** wanted to do. To get to that point, I had to give up my scientific concept of a "good group," remind myself that this group was different and had its own agenda, force myself to become interested in and curious about that agenda, and realize that my job was to understand that agenda and help them achieve it. This realization was paradoxical because in **accessing my ignorance** and becoming curious, I was actually being a better scientist than when I was imposing what prior research had shown to be what a good group should look like.

- A second powerful lesson was that I could make a small change in their **process** that would have a big impact on their ability to manage the content. I often thought that this meeting was where I invented the concept of Process Consultation (Schein, 1969). As I look at it now, it was a clear case of HC. I humbled myself to their needs, allowed myself to get curious, wanted to help them, and then found an effective adaptive move unconsciously.

- My help did not hinge on special expertise. I was functioning more as a catalyst at the flipchart and was illustrating something that they could do for themselves. It is worth noting that this occurred in the late 1960s when group facilitation and the use of flipcharts was only slowly replacing the blackboard and people taking their own notes. The group quickly adopted the procedure of having one of them go to the flipchart at subsequent meetings and tracking the discussion, with equally good results. I was achieving one of the important helping goals of facilitating, **learning how to learn**.

HOW NOT TO CONSULT WITH DEC: THE MAC PROJECT

I close this section on DEC with two failures: Management Analysis Corporation's (MAC's) inability to help DEC and my inability to help MAC. Toward the end of the 1960s, as DEC was growing rapidly, Ken Olsen decided that having an outside consulting firm "take a look at us" made sense. There were enough strategic issues floating around that it seemed wise to Ken and the Operations Committee to bring in some management consultants to diagnose the situation and maybe make some recommendations.

MAC was a highly respected Cambridge consulting firm consisting of full-time consultants working closely with principals who were Harvard Business School professors and partners in MAC. The DEC project was to be coordinated by Professor Vancil and was to examine DEC's organization. Ken asked me to be helpful to MAC and to facilitate whatever coordination might be needed.

Over the next several months, MAC did a thorough job of interviewing senior management and analyzing the data. In my role as liaison with the MAC project team, I sat in on the sessions where they analyzed the interviews to reach a diagnosis and develop their recommendation. As a strategy consultant, MAC felt they had to make a recommendation to fix all the problems they saw. They concluded that the primary solution for DEC was to appoint and empower a strong Marketing VP. I tried to argue that, given what I had learned about the DEC culture, making *any* recommendation might be a problem. I suggested that MAC should instead focus on clarifying the problems and the costs of not fixing them but let DEC wrestle through them to its own solution. DEC managers, with their academic orientation, did not like anyone telling them what to do, as I had found many times over, but they did listen to data. Tell them what will go wrong if they don't centralize marketing; stimulate their thinking.

I also pointed out to the MAC group that DEC had tried various people in senior marketing roles, but they always undermined them because deep down they distrusted marketing, symbolized by the remark Ken made that "marketing is just lying to people instead of solving their problems." The MAC consulting company culture, however, demanded that a structural recommendation be made, or "We did not do our job." Professor Vancil and I debated this issue at length, but he was convinced that the recommendation for a Marketing VP made so much sense and was so well backed up by the data that it clearly would be proper to make the recommendation first and then back it up with fifty or so transparencies that would make the case.

The MAC people worked for hours to make the presentation outstanding, and they rehearsed it so that it would be obvious how the recommendation had been reached. Vancil assured me that I did not know how consulting worked and therefore rejected my proposal and invited me to "watch us work and learn." Though Ken had wanted me to be helpful to them by being a liaison, clearly MAC neither needed nor wanted my help. I learned that if someone does not want help, there is little you can do to get them to accept it.

When MAC indicated that they were ready, the Operations Committee gave them a two-hour slot at the beginning of one of their regular meetings. Professor Vancil and one of his MAC colleagues were set with their overheads presentation and, in the best tradition of management consultants, led with their primary recommendation—the creation of the Marketing VP. Ken Olsen listened politely for a few minutes and then, before more than one or two of the overheads could be presented, thanked the MAC group for their work and dismissed them! I was shocked at the abruptness but not surprised, given my own experiences with trying to tell DEC things.

Various detailed written reports were later provided to DEC, and individual managers concurred with much of what MAC had learned, but the primary recommendation went nowhere, and the power of all the data was lost in the shuffle. A few weeks later, Ken Olsen wrote a long memorandum to Vancil terminating the MAC contract. The letter basically thanked MAC for its efforts but noted that most of what MAC said DEC already knew.

LESSONS

■ In retrospect, what MAC had done was to treat DEC's "problem" as a simple technical structural issue for which a simple solution was the obvious answer. They had not noticed that the DEC culture of empowering managers and giving them lots of autonomy, combined with a founder who was reluctant to give up absolute control, made the empowerment of a single Marketing VP impossible. DEC had in fact tried that and found that the person in the job was undermined by both product managers and Ken himself. The DEC culture was a complicated matrix in which all major problems that required a decision were a priori complex and messy. Somehow the Level One interviews had completely missed this.

■ I had formed a Level Two relationship with Ken, which made it quite natural that he would ask me to be a liaison with MAC, but there was clearly no Level Two relationship between Ken, who was the client, and MAC's principal consultants. They took the project and ran with it on the basis of their "professional" understanding of what good Level One consulting is. Ken had told them I would be liaison and would help, but that was an offer, not a response to a request by MAC. They had not heard the implication of Ken's offer, namely that I knew a lot about the DEC culture and how to work within it.

■ I tried to form a Level Two relationship with Professor Vancil, who was the official head of the MAC project, by offering to reveal what I knew about DEC. Not only did he decide to ignore what I knew about the DEC culture, but he specifically told me that I did not understand consulting, that my views of DEC's resistance to being told what to do was irrelevant in the face of his overwhelming case, and, by implication, that I should learn from watching MAC perform. Vancil clearly did not want a Level Two relationship with me, which illustrated clearly for me that a relationship works only when both parties are willing to be at the same level.

■ I also learned from this experience that clients already know a lot of what outsiders bring to them, and some don't want to be told what they think they already know, while others hire the consultant to confirm what they know and plan to do. That way, if it goes wrong, they can blame the consultant. It is these perceptions that feed all the negative humor about consultants telling you the time by studying your watch. Furthermore, the client's failure to act on what they "know" and/or to accept the recommendations of the consultants results not from ignorance but from incompatibility between what the existing culture will allow and what the recommended solution is. An organization can only do what is consistent with its culture, a point that was completely missed by the MAC diagnosis and recommendation.

■ I learned that "being professional" and "keeping appropriate distance between the helper and the client" can be a terrible trap. I am especially suspicious when a boss tells me that his subordinates always tell him the truth because it is their "professional responsibility." I have heard surgeons claim that their nurse and tech would always tell them if something was wrong and have had that same nurse tell me "No way."

■ Minimal harm was done in this case, and there are undoubtedly work situations and helping situations where it is not necessary to develop Level Two trust and openness. But even here, it seems to me that it would have been safer to have a Level Two discussion between Vancil and Ken in which the groundwork could have been laid for at least listening to the presentation. Unfortunately, there was little further communication between Vancil and me, so I never found out what MAC's reaction to their dismissal was.

CASE 4. Implementing a New IT Technology in Bank Operations

This case taught me some important lessons about how difficult it is to define a problem clearly and solve it when the situation is complex, messy, and constantly changing. I was brought into the bank by Carlos, who had been a Sloan Fellow at MIT and had done his thesis with me, so I knew him very well. When he became a senior VP of International Operations of one of the largest US banks, he asked me to come to New York on a regular basis to "help me become a better manager by attending my meetings, observing me, and giving me feedback and advice on how to run a better operation."

Our relationship thus began with me coaching an individual executive and, by implication, his group of immediate subordinates. I would spend up to a day a week visiting his organization, sitting in on his meetings to provide whatever help I could to make him and his group more effective. The problems that the group generated were the typical ones of agenda management, participation, and decision making. I would provide occasional feedback during the meetings and then review Carlos's style with him after the meeting. Whereas Ken Olsen at DEC had left me to my own devices, Carlos was much more dependent, counting on me to help him improve his skills and help his group become more effective by frequently inquiring how he was doing and how the group was doing.

Carlos was my primary client, but I had to get to know the group as well in order to be helpful. In getting to know the group members individually and collectively, I always aimed for a Level Two relationship. Carlos also asked me my opinions about specific members of his team, something that I had warned him I would not do because I was not an expert at assessing individuals. If he insisted, I would turn this into a coaching session by asking him to talk out his own evaluation and help him to clarify his own assessment of his people.

THE NEW INFORMATION SYSTEM

Carlos decided to implement a new information system that would replace all the paper files that his fifteen clerks used for all their overseas transactions. Each of the clerks worked with five to ten banks and financial institutions all over the world and used one manila folder for each of those customers. As requests for money transfers came in, they would pull those files, riffle through the material, and then make the transactions on their desktop computers.

The new IT system to be implemented was part of a much larger program of updating the operations functions of the bank by replacing most of the paper files. The system allowed clerks to see several documents on the screen at one time so they could work on several cases at once without having to pull files all the time. To use the new system, the clerks had to enter all their paper file information into the new system.

Carlos then asked me to observe and interview the clerks to identify possible sources of resistance as they were sent off to training for the new system. I had by that time gotten to know most of the people and was trusted as a "helper," not a management spy. I suddenly found myself in the midst of a planned change project and could observe directly what could go wrong. For example, in order for the clerks to be working with several clients at the same time, they first had to learn to enter all the information on each client into the system and then learn how to bring up several pieces of information simultaneously. The manila folders were to be thrown away once all the information was in the system. However, it took a long time to learn how to do all this, and the clerks felt they never had enough time to both learn the new system and get all their routine work done as well. They varied hugely in their ability to adapt to the new system.

Even after the clerks had been officially trained, I saw many clerks secretly continuing to hold on to paper files, which they claimed were easier to manipulate than the computer screen. None of this had been anticipated, and Carlos dealt with it in a typically managerial way by insisting that the practice of using the paper folders should stop, but he was not enforcing the directive. Carlos wanted to be a "nice manager," and I could see the dysfunction in what he was doing, but I also knew that the paternalistic culture in which Carlos had grown up made his style something that I could not challenge directly without deeply offending him.

LESSONS

- I saw an instance of what I had read about in planned-change programs—if you don't involve the people who have to make the change in the planning of how it will be accomplished, they will find it difficult to do and will resist it in various ways.

- I also learned that the client sometimes does not have an accurate sense of when to ask for help. Instead of deciding to implement the IT system and **then** asking me to help, Carlos should have asked me what kinds of things might come up before he made the decision. We now had to deal with the diversity of talent in the group for this kind of computerized work and the various forms of resistance that emerged. And as it turned out, Carlos was not the kind of manager who could enforce his directives.

THE EMERGENCE OF SUPERCLERKS

It then developed that some clerks really liked the system and could do much more work on the computer as they got comfortable with the system, leading Carlos and the IT people to decide to create a small cadre of "superclerks" who could do all the work, which of course made many other clerks redundant. Carlos then asked me to help him figure out how to retrain the redundant clerks, because he said that the bank had a no-layoffs policy that was strongly implemented by his immediate boss. The superclerk idea could not be implemented until the redundancy problem was solved. Various efforts were made to retrain or out-place the redundant clerks, but months went by without any substantial progress. The superclerks and the regular clerks worked side by side while efforts continued to reduce the size of the pool.

LESSONS

■ My client revealed sides of himself that I had not been aware of, because, up until then, no circumstances had arisen that would test him. Carlos was not aware of the bank's no-layoffs policy and had not counted on his boss being completely committed to it. Carlos was also the kind of manager who would not challenge his boss on such matters, so he just slowed the project down while he tried to find ways of retraining the people.

■ I found myself playing a variety of different helping roles. With the clerks I was observing, asking them questions, and occasionally making a suggestion. With Carlos I was being a coach and educator to get him to see some of the unanticipated consequences of his decision to implement the new system. With respect to the IT project, I found myself in the middle of it as a participant and pawn adapting as best I could to new circumstances as they emerged.

A NEW BOSS AND A SURPRISE

Sometime during the second year of this project, Carlos's boss left and was replaced by a new boss, who, as he looked over the project's struggles to become productive, suddenly announced that the bank did not, in fact, have a no-layoffs policy and that they should go ahead with installing the superclerks, retraining those who could be retrained and firing the others. Surprise, surprise, the no-layoffs policy that we had been taking for granted had either been just the personal values of the previous boss, or the bank had put into effect a major policy change that Carlos was not aware of. In any case, none of this had been anticipated or planned for.

Carlos then wanted me to help him and his task force finish the design of the new job of superclerk, decide how many clerks to keep, and make plans for laying off the ones who would be redundant. I had learned from my experience with DEC that things can change unexpectedly, but I had never before encountered a situation in which the changes had such a direct impact on what my client wanted to do. Nor had I worked with a manager who was so ready to go along with what his bosses and his expert helpers, the IT people, wanted. Had I seen any of this coming, I would have spoken up, but it happened with little warning and required a quick next adaptive move.

DESIGNING THE CAREER OF THE SUPERCLERK

The new job, relative to the old clerical job, required a much higher-level employee in terms of skill level and pay grade. That part was manageable, but it was not clear what the career path of these superclerks would be in the future. The old clerks were dead-ended in their careers and did not mind the relatively low pay and lack of promotion. They were well adapted to their role and position in the career system. But the superclerks would want advancement, and the task force could not figure out a way to advance them. The superclerks would become specialists, and the bank had no ladder for this. In fact, the bank had a highly rigid promotional and career advancement system up the managerial ladder that was strongly enforced by the human resource function. Very high-level individual contributors could be given special status and pay, but there was no mechanism for dealing with highly technical individual contributors in the middle.

When this lack of a career path was discovered by the task force, the whole superclerk idea was abandoned! The original clerks were retained and even permitted to use their paper files along with the computers! After about two years, we were using the new and the old systems together, but with much lower productivity because of the large number of clerks that had been retained. Apparently, this was okay with senior bank management because changing the clerks' career tracks, wages, and promotion system was not something they wanted to tackle. IT was extremely unhappy about this outcome, but they could not do anything about it. Carlos accepted it, and life went on.

LESSONS OF THE ENTIRE CASE

- Working with Carlos was always an adventure because there were always new things he wanted to work on and new conditions to be dealt with. Over three years of consulting there, I learned firsthand how problem definition and technical solutions are highly vulnerable to unanticipated technological, political, and purely personal circumstances like the sudden retirement of Carlos's first boss.

■ The biggest lesson was **don't second-guess the future**, and don't make assumptions about the causal forces that may be operating. You never see the whole system, so don't second-guess it either. In the traditional research model, the existence of the no-layoffs norm would have been a sufficient explanation of the observed phenomenon that a potentially useful technology failed to be adopted. Had this boss not left, I would never have learned that it was not a general bank norm, and that bosses had considerable leeway in how they dealt with technologically produced redundancy.

■ The discovery that the bank had no career paths for this kind of superclerk was a complete surprise to both Carlos and me. Low-level clerk specialists were easy to manage, and their careers were well understood. Superclerks of the kind that would be created by this technology would have to be better educated, would want more pay, and would be autonomous operators instead of under managerial control.

■ So what was really in the way of introducing the new technology was some deeper cultural problem with the entire sociotechnical system, specifically an inability to visualize and/or adopt a less hierarchical system in which bosses might play more of a consultant role to highly paid professional operators who, like airline pilots, might spend their whole careers in some version of this new role. In fact, the no-layoffs norm might have been a convenient rationalization to avoid having to change deeper cultural assumptions about the nature of work and hierarchy in this bank.

■ No great harm was done but not much useful change had occurred either, and as a helper, I had to be content with just helping Carlos deal with the various events that overtook both of us. I learned the meaning of an adaptive move as contrasted with a solution.

Chapter Summary and Conclusions

In this chapter I have reviewed the sociological reality that relationships in all societies and groups can vary from negative, hostile, and exploitative to highly intimate. Each of these levels has a variety of situational rules that govern how close or distant it is appropriate to be, what it means to be more or less personal, and what is appropriately public or private. Our normal relationships with strangers, what I am calling Level One, also include transactional and professional service relationships that are governed by cultural rules of appropriate professional distance.

When we get to know someone personally and can work with him or her on a more personal level, this is Level Two, which is essential for real help to occur. Level Two trust implies that we are willing to make promises and will keep them. Level Two openness implies that with respect to our joint task we will share all relevant information and will not lie to one another.

SUGGESTION FOR THE READER

To get an insight into your own and others' views of openness and trust, find some time with a friend or colleague and ask the following question: "When you ask others for help or some service, how do you decide whether or not you can trust them, whether or not they are telling you the truth?" Ask yourselves for concrete examples.

Next, ask yourselves how you would go about trying to figure that out, or what kind of conversation you might consider having that would make you feel you could trust them.

As you discuss this, do you begin to sense the difference between Level One formality and Level Two personalization?

FOUR

Humble Consulting Begins with the First Conversation

Building a relationship is a process that begins in *the initial contact* that the helper has with the client. Understanding the importance of the initial response applies to all forms of helping, coaching, and professional counseling. What the doctor or lawyer says in the very first conversation has the potential of freezing the relationship in Level One or beginning to personalize it toward Level Two. It can apply equally well to the manager meeting a new employee or a group chair meeting a new team member.

In this chapter I explore the various choices that the humble consultant has in her initial response in order to highlight what she could do to begin building the Level Two relationship. In my experience most helping situations that go wrong do so because of errors of omission or commission in the very beginning. That was clearly the problem in Case 2, the engineering lab interviews, where I leapt in without giving the question of how to get started the slightest thought. As the cases below illustrate, the right initial response can not only begin to build the relationship but can also be, paradoxically, *immediately helpful,* as was shown in launching the culture change process in Case 1.

In Humble Consulting there is no "exploratory conversation," or "contracting," or "scouting," or "diagnosis" because your initial response starts a conversation that, if it builds the relationship, will automatically produce the data you need in order to decide whether and how to get involved. All your energy, therefore, should go into creating that open, trusting relationship from the moment of first contact.

How Is This to Be Done? The HC Attitude— What the Helper Must Bring to the Party

Building a relationship begins with attitudinal preparation, a conscious process of building the right kind of mind-set. When the phone rings and you are about to engage a potential client, you have to be ready in a number of ways, which I am calling the "HC attitude." Think of it in terms of the three Cs—commitment, curiosity, and caring.

COMMITMENT: YOU HAVE TO BE EMOTIONALLY READY TO WANT TO HELP

Don't pick up the phone or accept a lunch date from a potential client if you are not emotionally prepared to be helpful. If you are responding just to see what might be out there, your indifference will show in the tone and pace of your voice, what you actually say, and in your body language if you are meeting face-to-face. Level One professional distance can actually *prevent* relationship building. Try not to worry about whether this will produce income or not; let your motive be to see if you can solve the client's problem. If not, you can at least say and do things that will make the client feel really helped right away.

CURIOSITY: YOU HAVE TO WANT TO KNOW "WHO IS THIS PERSON?" AND "WHAT IS THE SITUATION?"

If you are emotionally prepared but don't have a clue what this will be about, be genuinely curious, because that will make you an active, engaged listener from the moment you are in contact with the other person. Don't take the call or go to the meeting if you are not curious to find out what this is all about. If you are busy or preoccupied, don't make the contact. If you are not curious about what goes on out there and what others are experiencing and worrying about, get out of the helping business.

CARING: YOU HAVE TO GET PERSONAL AS QUICKLY AS POSSIBLE

Focus on the person and what the client-to-be says to you. Clear your mind as much as possible of preconceptions. It is very difficult not to project into a future situation your own expectations based on past experiences with similar situations. It is equally difficult not to focus your listening effort just on those things where you think you can be really helpful. Don't be a hammer just looking for nails. Concentrate instead on actually hearing what the client-to-be is trying to convey. In this regard I have found it helpful *not* to look up the company, not to look at all the literature that the potential client may have sent you; as tempting as that might be, I want to focus on what the client tells me personally in the here and now.

Doctors, lawyers, and managers have these same choices. The doctor can arrive at the bedside wondering whether this patient will be relevant to his specialty, or he can get curious about the person and ask "Where are you from?" or he can get curious about the situation and start with "Where does it hurt?"

How to Listen

How you listen to the first things the person says provides crucial choices. You have basically three choices, all of which qualify as intense, interested listening but have different consequences for relationship building:

Self-oriented listening. What am I hearing that I can connect to and be helpful on because it taps into my knowledge, experience, and skills? How does what the person says link to my motives, values, and needs? Will it be to my advantage to get involved here or not? Do I have time for this?

It is difficult not to start and remain in this mode. We think we can hear both what is relevant to us and what the potential client is talking about, but in my experience, if I am busy evaluating how the potential client's comment fits into my life space, I am not allowing my curiosity enough scope and will most likely not really hear what the client is after. Ellen Langer's question "What else is going on?" highlights that we are always able to process several aspects of our experience (Langer, 1997). The issue is what captures our primary attention—am I curious about what this call means for me, or am I curious about the person and the situation at the other end of the line? That leads to the second- and third-choice options.

Content-empathetic listening. You may want to focus your listening on what problem, issue, or situation the person is trying to convey to you and what problem elements should be considered in what the person is trying to convey. This is not the same as content seduction, where you begin to imagine immediately what you might do if you were in that situation and let your attention wander to those possibilities. Your primary attention, energy, and curiosity stay focused on trying to understand the nuances of the content of the client's situation in whatever way he is conveying it. You ignore tone of voice and various cues about the person and try to focus on the situation that the person is trying to convey. For example, the person says, "I am really worried about the low level of employee engagement in my organization." If you are content focused, you will ignore the "I am really worried" and just pay attention to the employee engagement issue. However, you can also choose, instead, to be person empathetic.

Person-empathetic listening. You can focus your listening on how this person is experiencing and feeling about the situation he is describing to you. Here your primary attention and curiosity are focused on the urgency conveyed in the tone of voice and whatever other cues you have available to decipher what might be going on with this person as he is describing the content of his situation. You may hear anxiety, anger, impatience, relief to be talking to someone about the situation; concern, testiness about having to talk to anyone about this; skepticism about whether any good will come of this; and so on. It is your choice whether to give primary attention to these cues as you listen and to focus your primary curiosity on the person instead of the situation.

The first responses you make will depend on which way you listen, so you should be clear in your own mind what your intentions are and be prepared to adapt quickly to what you actually hear. If you want to build a relationship, it will be especially important whether you choose to personalize around the content of what you are told or whether you choose to personalize around the person who is telling it. Either one may be helpful, but you won't know until you are in the situation.

Choices of How to Respond

The initial things you say or do should both encompass honoring the client and provide you necessary information. In other words, your initial responses have multiple purposes—to make the client feel comfortable about having had to ask for help, to get you some more information on what is going on, and to be as sympathetic and empathetic as possible so that even the first few interactions will be felt by the client to have been helpful. I have been amazed how often those first humble inquiry questions, assertions, or revelations, or even just my silent attentiveness, prove to be really helpful on the very issue that the client was calling about because they provided, at the minimum, an opportunity for the client to hear herself, or, if you say something, an opportunity to focus, reframe, or provide a different perspective.

Authenticity—humble inquiry or reaction?   There is an important difference between a pure Level One inquiry model, where you just try to get the client-to-be to figure things out, and the HC approach, where you try to personalize and open the door to a Level Two relationship. Therefore, you must be as open and honest and authentically yourself as is consistent with the situation.

You have an important choice here—whether to ask a humble inquiry type of question or to reveal something about yourself, or to give in to a reaction you may be having. In my previous writing, I advocated humble inquiry as always the first step, but I found myself realizing that this does not mean literally to always stick to asking questions but rather to always convey an attitude of inquiry and interest. Paradoxically, that attitude is sometimes best conveyed by saying something personal about yourself or giving in to an honest reaction, as I did in Case 1, that reveals to the client that you have heard him. The only principle is that you should remain committed to being helpful.

Types of questions—what to ask and how to ask it. It usually feels most natural to ask some questions, but it is crucial to be aware of how many choices you have as to the type of question you ask initially and the tone of voice you choose in how you ask your question. Whether you respond with humble inquiry, essentially saying "tell me more," or begin to influence the interaction with more focused questions will, of course, depend on how the client presents himself and the situation. In that regard I have found it useful to distinguish the different kinds of questions you can ask according to their intentions and consequences.

I developed a typology of questions early in my consulting career and find it useful to remember my choices before I leap into a response (Schein, 1999, 2009, 2013). The typology is built around the principle that initially the helper has to both make the client feel comfortable and get basic information from ground zero; hence, it is best to begin with humble inquiry—open ended questions to which you truly do not know the answer.

As the client says more, ideas and hypotheses and insights inevitably form in your head, and you begin to feel the need to focus what you learn on the issues you begin to see around the person or the situation that is presented. You may not feel you have an answer, but you will begin to want to ask questions that focus the client-to-be and therefore take him away from how he might have continued his story into content that you want to know more about to satisfy your curiosity. This category is diagnostic inquiry.

Diagnostic inquiry. Diagnostic inquiry is a broad category of questions that can vary from as little as "Huh," or "Say that again," or "Help me to understand this" to a pointed "Why did that happen?" or "What did you do then?" or "How did that make you feel?" What diagnostic questions have in common is that they influence the client's story, they force the client off her track in telling it, they alter the process by which the client chooses to reveal herself.

I call these "diagnostic questions" because they are designed to help both you and the client to begin to understand the situation or herself a bit better. If I sense that the client has much more to tell me on her own terms, I certainly will let her do that; but when either my need for specifics or her need to pause and get a reaction creates a break in the flow, I will ask a diagnostic question, knowing full well that I am now taking charge of the conversation to a certain degree by shifting from just listening attentively to appearing in the conversation as a person with my own interests. I have made it into a conversation rather than one person just telling another person a story.

Until I depart from humble inquiry, I am just an unknown entity in the conversation, little more than the interested listener. With a diagnostic question, I become a person with a point of view and have thereby begun to build the relationship in a certain direction. Diagnostic questions can be differentiated into three types:

- Conceptual—the basic question "Why?" which forces the client to think about and examine various aspects of what he has just told me and to think about causes

- Emotional—the basic question "How did that make you feel?" in reference to some event that the client has just talked about

- Behavioral—the basic question "What did you do?" in reference to some choice points in the client's story

These three types of questions can also be linked to a *time horizon*—what *did* you do, what *can* you do, and/or what *will* you do? Or what did you feel, what do you feel about this now, how will you feel about this in the future?

Circular questions and process focus. If the goal of your question is to help the client to see her embeddedness in a complex system, to think more deeply about what may be going on in the story she is telling, you can ask each of these types of questions in a form that family therapists call circular questions. In a circular question, you ask the client to speculate on how others in her system might be thinking, feeling, and/or behaving.

The most common occasion for this type of question in my experience is when a client asks me to visit her organization to interview her subordinates or take some other action that I am not comfortable with. I am then inclined to ask her, "If I show up and go ahead and do that, what do you think their reaction will be?" By that question I am asking the client to consider the possible consequences of what she proposed and to test for myself how much the client-to-be understands that everything the consultant does is an intervention with consequences. Depending on what the client-to-be says, we can then explore how she would announce my arrival, what she would tell the subordinates is the purpose of her bringing me in, how she would deal with the information gathered, and what her longer-range plan might be. This kind of questioning also begins to focus our conversation on process issues, how things are being proposed to be done, which in my experience will often turn out to be where the client needs help most (see Chapter 6).

Case 1 illustrates how I proposed immediately that the client visit me instead of my visiting them, and this worked well. In Case 2, the engineering interviews, my colleague and I just showed up and did our interviews without any consideration of how this might impact the lab, and this worked out poorly.

Diagnostic questions change the course of the conversation and invite the client to consider some other elements of her story, but they do not introduce new content into the conversation. When questions do introduce new content, I think of them as suggestive questions. In previous work I called these "confrontative," because they forced the client to look at new information that she may never have considered, but the HC attitude does not really ever condone what is implied in confrontation, so I feel that *suggestive* is a more accurate word in terms of what it connotes.

Suggestive inquiry. As a conversation with a client begins, we inevitably experience moments when our own ideas, feelings, and suggestions for action pop into our heads, and we have to decide whether or not to reveal those thoughts. Where the diagnostic question influences the direction of how the client tells his story, the suggestive question forces new content into the story, content that did not come out of the client's head.

The big question about this type of intervention is when to do it, knowing that you are asking the client to think about something that he had not considered initially and knowing that the most dangerous aspect of being the helper is to give premature advice and thereby to undermine your own credibility. The trap for the helper is that the client had considered it, ruled it out for various good reasons, and now wonders why the consultant has come up with such a bad idea. There is nothing more discouraging when you are trying to build up a relationship than to have the client say, "I already tried that. It doesn't work!" with the implication "How come you, the consultant, don't see all the flaws in what you have suggested?"

Putting the suggestion or idea into question form helps somewhat, and you can soften the tone if you are unsure. What rarely works is the recommendation that the consultant has worked out on her own after a period of so-called data gathering as the MAC project with DEC showed so dramatically (Case 3). What works better is to wait with the suggestive question until you feel that a Level Two working relationship has been achieved to some degree and you feel that the client trusts you.

Once I feel that the client and I trust each other at the working level, that we will be honest and open with each other on task-related matters, I feel completely comfortable in saying things like "Did that not make you feel angry?" or "Why did you withdraw instead of confronting the situation?" or "In the future, do you think you could go talk to the person?" or, as we will see in Cases 5 and 6, "Have you considered . . . ?" (something different than what the client's story had revealed or what the client proposed).

Process-oriented inquiry. Process-oriented questions come in three forms: redirecting how the client is formulating her analysis of the problem, redirecting what the client wants you to do in the helping process, and/or focusing on the interaction with the client in the here and now. In the cases I discuss below and elaborate on in Chapter 6, I redirected both how the client formulated the problem and what she wanted me to do to help her. Questions that focus on the interpersonal process that is occurring between the client and you in the here and now are likely to be less frequent but are always available if you are not comfortable with how the conversation is going.

As we look ahead to developing adaptive moves in complex, messy situations, redirecting the conversation and using more dialogic formats may become more necessary, as I show in Chapter 7. The purpose of such here-and-now questions is to make both parties aware that they are in a relationship-building process, and this process is itself subject to analysis and review. In your conversation with the client, you can always say, "How is this going?" "Am I being helpful?" "Is there something else I should be doing or asking you about?" "Are we okay?" or something similar.

Personal revelation. First, the HC attitude requires authenticity. You cannot fake it or evolve a role that hides your reactions. Let's revisit the dilemma of you wanting to use humble inquiry and stay in a questioning mode in order to learn as much as you can about what is on the client's mind, but now you have a strong reaction to something the client-to-be says in the opening. Should you voice it? I have found that the key here is whether you are reacting from a position of curiosity and/or empathy or whether you are reacting from self-orientation. Revealing something of your own personal reaction is clearly an invitation to get more personal, but if it occurs either because of self-orientation or before you have a sense of what is really on the client's mind, it has the danger of sending you down a diagnostic track that is your choice, not a choice that reflects what is really on the other person's mind. I would therefore be particularly cautious in revealing my reaction unless I felt that hiding it would be unauthentic.

Second, you have to continue to play within the cultural rules of what is or is not appropriate to share. I may be upset by the kind of voice the caller has and know that it is inappropriate to share that reaction, but I may also be upset by the condescending tone of voice he is using and feel it appropriate to find a way to voice that reaction. My blurting out in Case 1 "What did you do?" was technically a question but was really felt by all of us to be a helpful reaction because it showed commitment, curiosity, and caring.

Illustrative Cases

As the cases described below illustrate, once the client has responded to the initial pure humble inquiry, we already have reactions that force us to choose whether to just keep the story going with "tell me more" or whether to switch to diagnostic questions, circular questions, suggestive questions, process-oriented questions, or personal reactions and revelations.

CASE 5. Reframing Whether to Develop a Culture Analysis Template

This case illustrates how early diagnostic and suggestive questions led to a complete restructuring of a project proposed by the client.

Potential Client: *This is Marcia Higgins. I am the Communications Vice President for Company X. We are a*

*large international supplier of equipment to the oil industry.
Dr. Schein, we are wondering if you would help us develop a
template for analyzing our culture. We are growing very fast,
are hiring many new people in different countries, and are
concerned that we will lose our values. We have set up task
forces worldwide that are ready to do the culture analysis
and identify the key values that we do not wish to lose. Can
you help us build the template for this analysis?*

(I found this somewhat confusing and, worse, could
not see what they had in mind that they could not easily
get from any of my publications. But I was intrigued
and curious about the content, so I chose humble
inquiry to get more information.)

Ed S.: *Could you tell me a bit more about what you have
in mind?*

M. H.: *Well, we think, as we hire new people, it is very important to teach them the basic company values so that we do not
lose our culture. We want you to help us define these values
by giving us a template and a process for the task forces to
use to come up with the key values that can then be taught to
new employees.*

(As I am listening intently to the culture issue, I hear
something that sounds perfectly reasonable that I
could certainly agree to do. I could suggest a project to
begin work on defining the template. But I felt something was not entirely right about this, and it occurred
to me to wonder if existing employees were going to
teach company values to new employees, why they
needed a long diagnostic process to identify the values.
So I asked a further question that was really a hypothesis that I was checking and was therefore suggestive.)

Ed S.: *Don't the existing employees in each task force live these values now?*

M. H.: *Yes, of course, our employees are constantly reminded of them.*

Ed S.: *So they would be ready right now to teach new employees how things are done in your company?*

(I am, in effect, now suggesting a whole new process idea to check whether she has considered this alternative way of thinking. I am leading her toward a different way of formulating the problem and, at the same time, testing what is really on her mind.)

M. H.: *Oh, yes, but we thought it would be important to do a more thorough analysis of the culture and have some of those values written down formally.*

(I now face a major choice: to be *person* empathetic by asking why she thought it was so important to analyze the culture, or to be *content/situation* empathetic and ask about the values. I chose the latter because I thought it would lead to helpful action more quickly. But the reader should note that this was a critical choice point of whether to explore her feelings and reasons or move toward solving the problem of preserving the values.)

Ed S.: *Can you give me an example of such values?*

(*Asking for examples* often turns out to be the single most important intervention because until you have examples you don't really know what the client is talking about. So this is back to pure humble inquiry but around the situation, not her.)

M. H.: *Each team in the field counts on total dedication to the team and absolute loyalty, no matter what, for example.*

(Marcia's immediate ability to provide a couple of critical values gave me the insight that if we went ahead and I gave them a template, they would spend some unknown number of weeks or months with reviews by me to produce an "official" list of company values to be taught to newcomers. This could be a lucrative project for me, but I sensed that Marcia was really more concerned about newcomers being indoctrinated right away, and I did not see how a published list would really facilitate intense indoctrination at some point in the future.

I decided to try a more suggestive question that had in it an idea that made more sense to me, given the urgency I felt in the phone call. I could have just asked some more about creating the list and what they would do with it, but my honest feeling was to short-circuit all that and take a risk with suggesting something different, but still in question form.)

Ed S.: *Are you hiring people right now and in the next few months?*

M. H.: *Oh, yes, this is going on all the time, which is why we are in a hurry to produce the list of values.*

Ed. S.: *But, as you said, aren't the present team members in your task forces living these values all the time?*

(This was both a circular question, a test of whether my suggestion would work, and a lead-in to getting Marcia to consider what I was thinking about.)

M. H.: *Oh, yes!*

(I now had a better sense of what was really on her mind—getting new employees on board quickly and instilling the company values immediately. Why they felt they needed a formal process of identifying the company values and writing them down was suddenly even less clear, and I wondered whether that was her way of trying to involve me, since I had written the culture books. I began to switch my listening from focusing on content to focusing on her and her motives and decided to test the situation with a concrete suggestion.)

Ed S.: *Then why not have the task forces work directly on how they will indoctrinate newcomers, and, in that process, they will have to identify the key values that they want to uphold, like the ones you just told me. In order to teach them to newcomers, they will, in any case, have to learn to describe the values for themselves and to develop their own examples. Instead of putting energy into analyzing the culture, why not go directly to transmitting it? If the task forces are already set up, just ask them to evolve their indoctrination programs, which will force them to articulate the key values.*

M. H.: *Let me think about that; it is an intriguing idea. I will get back to you.*

(I was reacting to the urgency that I felt in Marcia's request and therefore decided to make a suggestion that would speed up what they wanted to do, to teach newcomers the company's values. The key to making this suggestion was my discovery from the earlier responses that they had task forces already in place to do the indoctrinating. I was suggesting a different task for the task forces. Everything so far had taken place in one phone call. A couple of days later Marcia did call back.)

M. H.: *Hello, Dr. Schein. Your idea is a good one and would get us moving much faster. But I have to check this new plan out with our CEO, and he will want to talk with you because this is a different approach. He comes to Cambridge often, so you two should meet on his next visit a week from now. He will be in touch.*

(I got an e-mail the following week saying that the CEO's trip had been canceled but that he did want to talk about this on the phone, which happened the next day.)

CEO: *Hello, Dr. Schein, Marcia tells me that you had a different idea about our project to identify key company values that have to be taught to new team and project managers.*

Ed S.: *Yes, it occurred to me that if you already had task forces of current employees set up, and these employees lived the company values, why not use them immediately as teachers of these values instead of going through a big diagnostic step to get the values written down. In any case, they can be written down later as they are learned and internalized. This would speed up the process and ensure that the present employees would themselves relive the values as they teach them to newcomers.*

(I was taking a chance here of going into the "doctor role" and revealing my own solution instead of asking the CEO to tell me what his goals were for this project. This would count as choosing to be authentic, since I was hooked by now on this solution and moving into *revealing* instead of further inquiry.)

CEO: *Well, that makes a lot of sense, and, now that I think about it, I believe that when Marcia and I first talked about it, that is what I had in mind, but she thought the documentation was a necessary step. I don't think so myself, so I am glad you brought that up. I believe we will go ahead on that basis. This was very helpful. Send us your invoice for time spent on this.*

(I was hugely relieved that this idea seemed to fit his priorities. I did not know how all this was sitting with Marcia, however. Had I killed her idea and created a problem between her and the CEO? A few days later I got a call from Marcia.)

M. H.: *I talked to our CEO, and he was very happy with this new direction. To tell you the truth, when he first asked me about this, I thought that my communications job required me to do the documentation of the values, that he would want this. But I had doubts about it myself and am much more comfortable going to work with the task forces to begin the training program for new employees.*

Ed S.: *Great. Why don't you try this approach, see how it works, and let me know sometime down the road how it is going.*

(I wanted to keep the door open to further adaptive moves if the indoctrination approach was not working and convey to Marcia that we had an open loop that could be used for further exploration of the issue if needed. I followed up with Marcia a couple of months later with an e-mail asking how things were going and learned that, in the end, they agreed on just three key values—absolute loyalty, total dedication to the project, and a 24/7 commitment to the project and the company. It turns out that the template and the period of formally describing their values would have muddied the waters because these three values were what they were really worried about losing.)

LESSONS

■ The basic help occurred in the very first conversation, when my curiosity and interest helped Marcia rethink what she was trying to do and reconsider her original request. It may have also occurred to her after this first conversation that she was being too self-preoccupied in thinking that as communications director it was her job to bring the list of cultural values into some general written form. It was this kind of experience that made me think of real help often being immediate and fast.

■ What of relationship building? My honest questions evidently conveyed to Marcia that she could be open with me and discuss the problem from the different perspective that I had brought up, a perspective that eventually made sense to her and to the CEO. We had been able to build up enough of a relationship on the phone for real help to occur. I concluded that being totally honest about my reactions was the right approach. I also learned that I could move from humble inquiry to being the suggestive "doctor" within a fairly short time if I felt from Marcia's and the CEO's tone of voice and content that she had been open enough with me and could hear a modification of what she wanted.

■ I gave up a potentially big project, but I believe that my approach to digging out what they needed and wanted was more helpful, and they clearly agreed. My questions tried to convey that I understood the problem but saw an alternative way to deal with it, and that I understood their sense of urgency. They could see that the energy in the task forces could be much better used to develop training and indoctrination methods for the newcomers that were coming soon, and that, in the process, they could construct lists of the most important values.

CASE 6. Creating a Client through a Process Suggestion—Alpha Power Company

This case is unusual because a *revealing* kind of response on my part in the first conversation led to a twelve-year client relationship. The story again began with a phone call.

M. M.: *Hello, Dr. Schein, this is Mary Myers. I am the head of HR for Alpha Power, and we are looking for a culture consultant. As you may know, we are currently on probation for some environmental violations a few years ago that led to a criminal indictment and a strong statement by the judge that the environmentally irresponsible behavior of the company was due to the "company culture."*

We have hired two environmental lawyers to deal with the legal aspects of the case and to help us develop a better environmental program. We think this does have a lot to do with culture, so we would like to find someone who could help us with the analysis of our culture problem. We thought you might have some colleagues or even graduate students who might be able to help us with this . . .

(As I listened I got quite interested because I did not have a regular client at the time and was intrigued by the prospect of working with a power company, having already begun to think about safety issues in the nuclear industry as a result of an invited talk to the

International Atomic Energy Agency on the cultural
issues in nuclear safety.)

Ed S.: *All that sounds very interesting and challenging. I don't
know of any colleagues or students at this time, but how
about me? I would be interested in this issue.*

(This was about as far as one could get from humble
inquiry, but it reflected my intense curiosity about
the organization and was an authentic spontaneous
response.)

M. M.: *Oh, no, we couldn't possibly afford you, . . . but I will
mention it to the CEO and the task force that is working on
this. So I will get back to you.*

(A week went by before the next call.)

M. M.: *Well, Dr. Schein, there was actually some interest in
getting someone at your level that could work with the two
lawyers as a kind of internal "environmental quality review
board" reporting to the main board. We would like to meet
with you to consider this further; can you come down to meet
with some of our senior executives next week?*

(I agreed, and we set a date. In this instance I did not
consider charging them for this time because I had
volunteered myself, and we were clearly in a mutual
testing phase, though they did volunteer to pay for
the expenses of the trip. The visit to the headquarters
was a cultural experience in its own right. Entering
the building involved an elaborate sign-in procedure;
waiting to be picked up required sitting in a very
formal, sparse reception room; and riding in the
elevator to the executive floors, I saw both pictures
of the history of the company and a television screen

broadcasting employee news and company values. I was finally shown into a large, well-appointed conference room, where the COO, the administrative head of all the company services, the head of labor relations, and Mary awaited me. They asked me about my work on organizational culture and described their situation with the judge and the probation.

I was intrigued and also acutely aware that the purpose of this meeting was to determine whether these key executives and I would mesh in some fashion. The conversation was informal and very general, with the understanding that they would discuss the visit, decide whether or not to hire me, and let me know through Mary at some future time. A week or so later, I got the call.)

M. M.: *Hello again, Dr. Schein, the group enjoyed their visit with you, and we have decided to go ahead with you as our culture consultant. Your direct contact will be Jim Stone, who is currently our director of Environment, Health, and Safety (EH&S), and who is charged with the program to get the company off probation. You will join the two lawyers and, with them, will report to the environmental committee of the board. You will be a member of the company's top-level committee of EH&S chaired by Jim. This committee is charged with creating and reviewing all EH&S programs and includes all the senior operating VPs and the COO. We also want you to meet our chairman and CEO on your next visit, because he has the longer-range perspective on how the company must get itself off probation. You should also know that there is a court-appointed monitor who has full access to the company and who writes quarterly reports on the progress of the company for us and for the judge. We are very much looking forward to working with you.*

(This was a lot to take in at once, but it fitted roughly with what I wanted to get involved in because of the safety angle. Thus began a relationship with Alpha that lasted twelve years and educated me to the difficult dynamics of a major urban power company and to the whole field of safety management. In many ways my relationships with various executives and employees in this organization highlighted the need for frequent adaptive moves as new issues around safety kept coming up.)

LESSONS

- Relationship building requires personal honesty. Once I realized that this could be a fascinating project, especially given my growing interest in safety, it would have felt insincere not to mention my interest in taking the consulting role myself.

- In my initial meetings with the Alpha executives, I was acutely aware that I was in a selling role, given that I really wanted this consulting assignment. This made me appropriately nervous, given that I was way out of my HC role, but I was also aware that my talks to the international nuclear energy agency gave me some credibility and confidence that I had something to contribute. In a sense, I was a bit of an expert with respect to how the safety issues that Alpha said it had were likely to be intertwined with cultural forces in the company.

- The whole experience made me highly aware of how you have to be prepared to shift roles as your own needs, as well as what is learned from the client, change the nature of the situation. This experience also showed me the complexity of client systems, which I explore further in Chapter 7.

How to Begin Personalizing Immediately in a Group Situation

Group meetings can have at least three different levels of relationship. I have seen work groups run by *Robert's Rules of Order* that are clearly designed by their founders and chairs to stay at Level One. Members are expected to play by the rules and to stay in their various roles. Personalization would be considered inappropriate and a waste of time. Whether or not a group needs to go beyond this level depends on the task the group is trying to accomplish and the degree to which that task requires coordinated actions by the group members. The higher the interdependency, the greater the need for Level Two trust and openness. Under some conditions teams do aspire to reach even Level Three, as in the case of Navy Seals or other groups that are totally interdependent and work in extremely unsafe conditions where *intimate* knowledge of one another's reactions is necessary.

Many kinds of work groups are teams in name only because what each member actually does is independent of what others do. Being physically near one another does not make a group a team, nor does reporting to the same boss. What makes a team is task or emotional interdependence. If the task is not analyzed and the interdependencies are not identified, there is no way of knowing at what relationship level the group should operate. However, how we begin is again crucial, as the next two cases, one a success and one a failure, illustrate.

CASE 7. Mass Audubon Board Task Force— A Personalization Success

The Massachusetts Audubon Society (Mass Audubon) is a large, successful conservation organization that has been operating for a long time throughout New England creating sanctuaries, protecting bird nesting areas, acquiring land adjacent to such areas, and running a variety of educational programs to educate children about nature. I had been on the board for about two years when Norma, the head of Mass Audubon, and Louis, the chair of the board, decided that it was time for a capital fund-raising campaign. Such a campaign had been run a decade or more previously, and the needs for new buildings and expansion of the programs was growing rapidly.

Because of my organizational background I was part of a "committee on board process" that met monthly to examine how the board did work and should work to make the organization effective. It was in those meetings that the question of launching a new capital campaign came up. The big question was whether the board was ready to tackle such a campaign, because it would require a great deal of extra work and commitment from the board members.

The process committee decided that we needed to create a task force of committed board members to address the question of whether or not we were ready and asked me whether I would be willing to chair this task force. I agreed and took it as a challenge to see whether using Humble Consulting ideas could influence how this task force of ten individually selected board members would work together.

Norma, a couple of board members on the task force, and I were meeting to decide how best to launch the task force. I was faced with a dilemma right away because Norma asked me to give her airtime at the first meeting to tell how the previous capital campaign had made a number of errors that she wanted to forewarn us about. I thought about this and decided it would get us off on the wrong foot, so I asked Norma to give me leeway as the chair to run that first meeting in my own way. She grumbled a bit but was now stuck because she had asked me to be the chair.

What was on my mind was a number of recent experiences I had had with the type of dialogue that had been proposed by Bohm (1989) and was being evolved by Bill Isaacs (1999). First, I suggested that our initial meeting should be over a meal, preferably at a nice club or restaurant. Norma thought this was an unnecessary expense, but before I could argue, one of the other members at the planning meeting offered to support such a dinner at his Boston club. So that was settled to my satisfaction. My plan was to let the group get acquainted informally over a meal with only the vague mandate that we would be discussing whether or not the board and the organization were ready for a capital campaign.

My key intervention to personalize this issue was to adapt a process I had learned in the various dialogue groups—to have a formal "check-in" before starting the dialogue itself to ensure that everyone's voice had been heard and that a first "group act" had been completed. I asked Norma and Louis not to say anything formal until I had completed our check-in. I had a particular form of check-in that I wanted to try.

MY ADAPTIVE MOVE

Just after coffee and dessert had been served, I called the group to attention and said the following:

"To get our discussion going I would like to ask us all to do something that some of you might find a little different, but I consider it very important to start in this way. I would like each of us, in the order in which we are sitting, starting to my left, to take a minute or two to tell us, from the heart, why you belong to Mass Audubon. I would like no discussion or

interruptions until we have heard from all of us. We can then
proceed with our formal agenda. This will take us a while but
it is important that we hear this from everyone. Roger, why
don't you begin? Why do you belong to this organization?"

The logic behind doing this kind of check-in was to
get everyone to say something introductory even though
the group members knew one another from being on the
board. The logic of choosing to ask people to talk "from
the heart" about their membership was to *personalize* that
membership and, at the same time, to gather necessary
information based on what people said and with what
intensity, from which we could infer how committed the
members of this task force might actually be to a capital
campaign. If enthusiasm in the task force was weak, we
would have to consider postponing the whole idea.

What happened could best be described as "magical."
Each person, especially Norma and Louis when they took
their turns, spoke with great passion about how important
Mass Audubon was in his or her life, how important its
role was in conservation and nature education, and how
enthusiastic each one felt about helping the organization
grow and prosper. By the end of a half hour, everyone had
spoken, and we knew that this task force was ready to proceed with the details.

As I could observe, and as was confirmed later in conversation, the unanticipated benefit of asking everyone this
question was that Norma and Louis for the first time heard
in detail how committed the board members of this task
force were. It was important that each person had spoken
with feeling and had given details of his or her commitment, because that provided information to Norma and
Louis that they did not have from just knowing these same

people in their board meeting roles, where they often spoke very little.

As the planning developed over the next months, we realized that the next issue was whether the staff of the organization would be ready to do the extra work that a capital campaign inevitably entailed. Instead of second-guessing this, my task force decided that the first event at our dinner had been so meaningful that we should do something comparable with the staff. We decided to have a lunch meeting of fifteen or so senior staff at which we repeated a version of what we had done at our dinner. I said that all of us would check in at the beginning of the meeting by telling why we belonged to Mass Audubon, and the members of my task force would go first. Then each staff member would give his or her answer until all of us in the room had spoken. We again found a heartening level of support for the organization and the capital campaign.

We learned later that one of the most significant unanticipated outcomes of that meeting was that for the first time the staff actually heard ten board members say why they belonged to Mass Audubon. Until that time the staff saw these board members as only names with unknown levels of interest in the organization. Furthermore, as we had anticipated, the staff for the first time learned a great deal about one another's levels of commitment and interests. The organization had been plugging along at a Level One formal-role-determined process and had never really had a session where more-personal feelings, motives, and values could be shared.

The question in a group setting of "Why do you belong to Mass Audubon?" was carried forward to other staff meetings and became an important starter to many of the working meetings that followed. What started out as a relatively minor intervention, in terms of time taken, turned out to have major impact because it personalized the whole process of working together on the capital campaign. The campaign itself took off with great enthusiasm and over its two-year period successfully met its multimillion-dollar target.

LESSONS

■ When I first decided to open our task force with this check-in process, I had an intuition about having everyone say something that would be personal and, at the same time, would engage emotional commitment. I did not realize, however, that choosing that particular question opened the whole group up to more of a Level Two set of relationships, which turned out to improve communication between the board members and Norma. What had been previously a cordial but formal relationship now became a more trusting relationship in which board members felt more open in telling Norma how they really felt.

■ I learned that if you **impose** a structure you are running a risk, but the results are sometimes important enough to warrant taking that risk. I was willing to run the risk of being seen as too touchy-feely by asking people to speak from the heart and insisting that we hear from everyone before allowing questions, reactions, or any form of discussion. I was imposing a process that was both an invitation to personalization and, at the same time, a preliminary test of whether this group had the energy and passion to move forward. By asking people to speak from the heart, I was inviting an emotional response

because I thought we all needed to calibrate one another
at this level.

■ The essence of the adaptive move was to change the
nature of the conversation, which may turn out to be
the most important way to deal with complex, messy
problems.

CASE 8. The Cambridge-at-Home Committee— A Personalization Failure

A group of friends and acquaintances formed a group
to explore the concept of staying in our houses as we
aged rather than going into a nursing home. After a few
social meetings in which we spoke about the concept in
general terms, we decided that it was feasible and turned
ourselves into more of a working group that would make
"Cambridge-at-Home" an organizational reality. I was one
of the more active members, and the group knew that I
had a group and organizational background, so it was no
surprise that I was asked to chair the group, even though I
was not one of the original founders of the group and, for
that reason, had somewhat less status.

I realized that our group of eight members had different
skills, different levels of involvement, and different expectations, so I decided to be highly laissez faire in letting members who had something to say have their full opportunity
to say it. I was, in effect, encouraging a movement toward
Level Two on the presumption that a volunteer group like
this would not function well unless the members got themselves personally involved. I was pushing personalization
through listening carefully to people and giving whoever
had an opinion the floor for as long as he or she needed
it, especially if the subject was germane to our task. For

example, there was a lengthy debate about what pictures
should be put on the brochure that would announce our
group and the project. One member was particularly
adamant and took up a lot of airtime, which I allowed him
to have because I thought his involvement would be crucial
down the line.

After one meeting when this member had taken a lot
of time, I received an e-mail from one of the founding
members accusing me of being a terrible chair in "allowing
meetings to ramble and encouraging members to drone
on who had nothing to contribute." He alleged that I, of all
people, with all my alleged knowledge of groups was showing my "complete incompetence" in how I was chairing
this committee. He complained to several other founding
members, which led to a separate discussion between me
and two of these other members to consider what to do.
I explained to them why I was chairing the way I was, "in
order to allow members to feel that they were each heard
so that they would become appropriately involved, as we
needed their commitment later."

In this conversation I learned an important cultural
lesson. The two members with whom I was having this
conversation were experienced board members of various volunteer and arts organizations in Cambridge and
Boston. They told me in a friendly but firm way that they
understood very well what I was trying to do but that most
of the group was not used to this level of openness and
really preferred the discipline of a more traditional way of
running meetings. Though we each had a role to play in the
group, we were not really interdependent and did not need
the level of personalization that I had been trying to reach.
I had erred in not analyzing our task because, had I done
so, I would have realized that efficient, crisp meetings were

what they were used to and what would adequately meet the needs of the task.

We also discussed another dynamic that was operating, namely that the person who had criticized me so severely was probably upset that he had not been named as chair in the first place. At the time he was our official treasurer and was well embedded in that role, so no one thought of giving him the chair. When he saw me mismanaging, from his point of view, he quite rightly complained in the only way he knew how—by attacking my style as chair.

We resolved this issue by looking for an opportunity to restructure the group. We were now into a second year, had acquired some funding, and were clearly in a new phase. The founders who had discussed the leadership dilemma with me proposed that we now give the complaining founder the chair with the face-saving explanation that "I had been the appropriate chair to *get us started,* but now that we were seriously in business, we needed someone with financial experience and contacts to chair the group." He happily took over, ran a tight set of meetings, and, as far as I could tell, the group was happy with this resolution and functioned well from that point on.

LESSONS

■ My attempt to personalize, by giving everyone who wanted it all the airtime they needed, wasn't what a group like this needed or wanted. We were not that inter-dependent, so shutting down the long-winded members seemed to be okay with everyone. I had tried to help but had not inquired of the more senior members what kind of help was needed. I had played doctor, misdiagnosed, and provided the wrong pill. At the same time, I was

told that taking the initiative to get the group started
by accepting the chair was essential to get the project
started. I had been right to move into the leadership
vacuum. The group found that intervention quite helpful.

■ A second lesson was that an activity or behavior that is
out of line with the existing culture will not survive. As
chair, I had imposed an open style of running meetings
that maximized individual participation in order to further
my own goal of building commitment by fully hearing and
supporting every member. Most of the other members of
the group were used to more-formal, disciplined meetings, did not have some of the experiences I had had as
a group facilitator, and, most important, were probably
not interested in having Level Two personal relations in
this group.

Summary and Conclusions

This chapter focuses on how important it is to start building a Level Two relationship from the initial interaction. I
emphasize that this process begins with your commitment
to helping, your curiosity, and your caring for the client-to-
be. If you are self-oriented and listen for what the relationship might mean for you, the client-to-be will sense that and
either become dependent or aloof, remain in a Level One
relationship, and not reveal what is really on her mind.

The building of that relationship begins with what you
say, your tone of voice, and your attitude toward the other
person. Those actions will determine what the other person
says, which, in turn, will determine what you say next, and
so on in an interactive "dance" that leads you and the other
person to make implicit decisions about whether or not you

can work together, trust each other, and be appropriately open with each other.

You manage your end of this dance by your choice of the responses you make, which can range from humble inquiry to strong suggestions. In between these extremes, you can ask a variety of diagnostic questions dealing with causal analysis, emotional reactions, or actions taken. These questions can be past, present, or future oriented. You also have the choice of asking circular questions in which you invite the other person to speculate on how others might react to something. Finally, you have the choice of asking process-oriented questions that focus you and the other person on the process of problem formulation, on how the person wants to proceed, or on the relationship itself.

As many of the examples I have given so far indicate, even the early conversations often provide useful help in giving the client new perspectives, new frames for thinking about her problem, and new ideas that turn out to be really helpful.

SUGGESTION FOR THE READER

A potential client calls you with a question. Please look at all of the responses shown below and rank order them from the one you would be most likely to make to the one you would be least likely to make and ask yourself, "Why would I say that?"

Client on the phone: *Professor Schein, . . . glad I caught you. We would like to explore with you doing a culture survey for our organization. We think we have a problem of employees being too disengaged and want to find out what our culture is in this regard . . .*

1. Ed S.: Thanks for calling. I would like to help but wonder if you have considered the impact of doing a survey at this time.

2. Ed S.: Thanks for calling. Can you tell me what you mean by "too disengaged"?

3. Ed S.: Be glad to help, I have several surveys in mind that get at these issues, so let's get together and sort it out.

4. Ed S.: Sure, employee disengagement is an important problem. I think I can help. When can we meet to discuss this?

5. Ed S.: What sort of survey do you have in mind?

6. Ed S.: Tell me more . . .

7. Ed S.: Why would you want to do a survey? Why do you think this is a culture issue?

8. Ed S.: What is on your mind? What's bothering you?

Now pair up with a friend or colleague, compare your answers and reasons, and then see if you can agree on what the possible consequences are of each kind of response and under what conditions you would use it. The goal of the exercise is to see if you can forecast the possible consequences of each of the above responses. There is no right answer or score sheet because what you say depends on the attitude with which you approach the phone call.

FIVE

Personalization: Enhancing the Level Two Relationship

Personalization is the fundamental process by which we move from being strangers to becoming acquainted, getting friendly, being teammates, getting connected, and in various other ways developing the higher level of trust and openness that I am calling a Level Two relationship. Sociologically, it is the process of abandoning to some degree the façade that we have all learned to wear in public and when we are in our official roles. It is the process of getting off the podium and letting our audience take a peek backstage. Personalization is telling one another a bit of our story of who we really are, where we have come from, and where we are going. It is letting each other witness how we do things when we are off duty, relaxing, away from the formality of work roles.

Personalization is a process that can only occur in degrees, and it can become dangerous. If we reveal too much of ourselves and our private backstage operation, we make ourselves too vulnerable to being taken advantage of or being humiliated or being "found out," like the Wizard of Oz, as not being able to support the claims we make in public. Personalization is especially dangerous when it occurs across formal hierarchical or status boundaries, because even in small steps like eating and drinking together, we are temporarily putting ourselves on an equal footing and can ask one another questions or say things to one another that in the Level One context might be considered offensive and disrespectful.

If we want to maintain distance, we should avoid getting into informal situations like meals, and we should always appear "in uniform" to signify our status and role, as in the case of the doctor in the white coat. Some Outward Bound training programs found that getting team members to tell one another a lot of the details of their private lives during their shared adventures, while interesting at the time, was later regretted and led to unanticipated tensions in the team. The participants had taken personalization too far into family and other areas that had nothing to do with their work roles.

Staying at Level One can feel safe and comfortable because the setting and the role relations are predictable. If your doctor said, "Let's go for a walk and have a chat," you would suddenly find yourself in unpredictable territory. You might be anxious, or you might be pleased, or you might be angry because you wouldn't know whether you were being charged for it, but in any case you would not know what was going on. Getting to know someone at a more personal level is a process of learning, it does not happen automatically, it happens in stages, and it is a series of tests. If we reveal more of ourselves, will we still be comfortable with each other? If I say what is really on my mind, will the other person be shocked or offended or unaccepting? How will I react to what another person tells me about herself? If I make myself vulnerable, will I be taken advantage of or humiliated? Given all of these dangers, why bother?

Why Personalize the Helping Relationship?

I argue that Level One helping works only when the problem is clear, when it has been clearly communicated to the helper, and when the helper has the requisite skills to solve the problem. I also argue that the organizational problems we encounter today are complex enough to prevent us from gaining initial clarity of what the problem is, or if hierarchical boundaries are involved, make it difficult for the subordinate or client to reveal what is really on his mind. Hidden assumptions about civility and norms about what is appropriate in a given role undermine communication. In those instances we need to find ways to personalize the situation to some degree in order to open up communication and find out what is really worrying the client and what to do about it. Some case examples will help make this clear.

CASE 9. Helping to Personalize Teaching at MIT

From 1969 to 1971, I was in a special job called "undergraduate planning professor." The Massachusetts Institute of Technology (MIT) was going through a period of change, so President Howard Johnson, the former dean of the Sloan School, asked me to help with various change efforts that were being launched in the undergraduate program. I was to be a free-floating change agent to work with various professors on innovations that they were trying to put in place in their courses.

What triggered these changes was the discovery that students were burning out by totally overworking in the competitive hothouse that the early undergraduate years had become. The catalyst was the discovery that students were not eating and were sleeping in the labs rather than going to their dorm rooms. By the time I got into this job, many of the changes were already under way, but Johnson felt that someone with change management skills would still be helpful to various professors implementing various innovations.

One of the major changes was to shorten the semester to end before Christmas so that the month of January could be declared an "independent activities period" (IAP) in which students were encouraged either to take time off or to do more recreational things that would provide relief from the classroom grind. This was presented to the student body with examples like "It's not okay to have formal graded activities during IAP, but if you want to go skiing with your professor, that is okay."

It might never have occurred to the social architects to call these changes "personalizing" the learning process, but that is what it was. The curriculum and the classroom had become too formal, and the administration recognized that students would learn more if the learning process could become more personal. One other structural change was to replace formal grading with the Pass/Fail/Incomplete option in some of the required freshman courses.

THE FRESHMAN MATH SECTIONS PROBLEM

I had an open door and invited students to come to me with complaints and concerns. A number of MIT freshmen complained that in their math sections the graduate assistant would come in, show the equations on the board, show how to solve them, ask for questions, and then give brusque technical answers. The students felt completely intimidated and were afraid to ask questions; if they did ask questions, they got short, formal answers that they often did not understand but were too afraid or embarrassed to admit that feeling. They wanted to feel more secure, to get to know the assistant more: where he came from, why he was in math, and how he found it so easy to do the problems (they were all men at that time).

I asked the assistants to meet with me, told them about the student complaints, and made a suggestion. I encouraged them to start the next section meeting by revealing something about themselves and explicitly encouraging the students to ask more personal questions in class. They resisted the suggestion at first as not being appropriate— they were the instructors, had to maintain their authority, and voiced the fear that if they did not maintain formal (Level One) distance, they might lose control of the classroom. However, they agreed to try in subsequent section meetings to tell the class a little bit about themselves, why they chose math, and how they too had struggled at first to understand some of it.

The results were immediate and dramatic. The graduate assistants reported that when they told the students more about themselves, they discovered not only that the sections became more relaxed and fun but that students actually learned more. Students could now feel more secure in asking "dumb questions" and reveal where their hang-ups were in trying to learn the math. The collective learning for us in the teaching seminar was that the higher-status person has to create the environment in which personalization becomes safe, and, in a sense, give permission for more open, trusting communication by *first revealing something about himself.*

LESSONS

■ I learned how trapped we can become in Level One formality, making all kinds of assumptions about how a given role should be performed. Our joint discussion, plus my suggestion of trying something different, served to give each of the assistants permission to try something new without violating the assumed norm. It is possible that if we had not done this as a group, each of them individually might not have had the idea or the courage to do something different. Collectively, we could agree to try some small adaptive moves to see what would happen.

■ I also learned that the formal work of learning is facilitated by the informality of a more-personal classroom and that the mechanism for this is the psychological safety that the student experiences. You have to feel safe to ask the dumb question and admit that you don't really understand. Only the higher-status person can make you feel safe.

BUILDING LEARNING COMMUNITIES IN PHYSICS

Two physics professors decided to experiment with pulling together a selected group of physics majors into a physically separated classroom and laboratory environment in which students would do everything together except living there overnight. I was recruited to work with one of these professors to help him build his community, especially to help him figure out what kind of a governance structure it should have and how much students should become involved in how the community ran.

I did not realize it at the time, but the issue was clearly how much personalization you can encourage when there are multiple levels of age, status, and rank involved and where the professors and assistants still have to evaluate and formally grade the students. As the community evolved over the sophomore year, it had to solve not only its internal processes of how to get along but also how to manage relations to the rest of the student body and MIT faculty as it evolved deeper levels of personal connection that other groups clearly did not have.

My main role was to observe, listen, and ask questions that would alert the professor to the issues that he had unleashed, then help him figure out how to deal with those issues. The toughest of these issues was how to deal with unrealistic student demands and discipline. I found myself frequently reminding the professor and his staff that if they really wanted student involvement, they would have to bring students into the governance structure of the community and give them a voice in how the community should create and manage the new norms of Level Two relationships across all the age, status, and rank boundaries. This learning community worked very well for many years but required the benign authority of the senior professor and his willingness to personalize relationships with his students.

LESSONS

- The hardest part for me and the other professors was to learn to listen to the students and actually hear them. Curiosity and desire to help were essential to this learning process on my part. I confirmed this a few years later in a special senior seminar that I was running for a small group of students who had earned the right to manage their own program. A very bright African American student admitted to this group, after we had become exceedingly open with one another, that his secret desire, which he had never admitted to anyone at MIT, was to become a ballet dancer. He had known this all along but never felt safe enough to reveal it. Once we knew this, we were able to help him make contacts with local ballet groups in Boston and send him to a highly successful career with one of the major companies.

- Once we give permission to break the coercive bonds of the role-related rules of Level One, it is amazing to discover how much we don't know about one another that is highly relevant to working together and getting the job done.

IMPROVING THE WORK OF A FACULTY COMMITTEE

My "home" was the Committee on Educational Policy, chaired by a professor of physics who was married to a professor of social psychology at another university, which made him quite aware of when and how he could use me. We spent many hours just talking over the whole change program within MIT and how this committee could contribute to the change efforts. After I had been on the committee for six months, he put me on the spot by asking me to take over one half-day meeting to run an exercise on how the committee could improve its own functioning.

I did not really know how to get these professors talking about themselves and group process. We were an extremely *Robert's Rules of Order*, task-oriented, formal, Level One group. Without knowing exactly where this would lead, I opened the meeting by distributing a one-page group evaluation questionnaire that asked each member to rate the group on each of ten group dimensions on a five-point scale of satisfaction. For example, how satisfied are you with how this group makes decisions? with participation levels? with depth of analyzing issues? and so on. I had put the ten dimensions on a flipchart with the five-point rating scale next to each dimension.

When everyone had finished their ratings, I said, "Okay, let's see where everyone has rated the group on dimension number 1," and asked each person in order to shout out his rating. I made it clear that I expected them to openly share their ratings. I used my process authority as temporary chair for that meeting to encourage openness. I then went on to dimension number 2 and so on until we had everyone's ratings on all ten dimensions on the flipchart in front of us.

From this point on, I did not have to say another word. The group jumped on these data like hungry lions and spent the next couple of hours doing a really magnificent job of analyzing what their own reactions meant and how they could use the results to articulate new norms for how this group should work in the future. I had stumbled on a process that professors were good at and enjoyed.

LESSONS

- I learned that you have to hook your change agenda to something that the change participants want to do, or at least know how to do. Analyzing how our committee worked might not have been chosen as a half-day agenda by the members had they been given a choice. But having to do it, they found it exciting and fun because I had given them a way of doing it that they were good at and enjoyed. I cannot imagine what my meeting would have been like had I just opened the meeting with "Our job this morning is to review how this committee works . . ." For one thing it would have been dominated by a few voices only and would have been awfully superficial. The data set gave equal voice to all members and got them started together in the analysis. In retrospect, it was important that I asked each member of the group to give his ratings out loud so that everyone had a voice at the beginning and the committee was tackling the data as one group.

Process reviews are essential to learning, but the group needs help in how to do them constructively.

■ Level One work groups and teams may wish to improve their functioning, but they don't have the conceptual tools to begin to know how to do that. Providing a set of dimensions like "decision making," "participation," and "leadership" may be necessary to get the group review process moving. The process tools can become important facilitators of personalization, just as eating together or playing games together can serve this function.

PERSONALIZING ACROSS CULTURES

My most enjoyable class over the years was the Sloan Fellows, upcoming young engineers and managers on their way to more senior corporate jobs, getting a masters degree or MBA in a two-year, full-time course. My part was the Friday morning class in organization studies. The program was particularly proud of the fact that as many as 40 percent of the Sloans were non-US nationals. These non-US Sloans had to speak English and were treated like the US Sloans in that they lived in the same neighborhoods, carpooled together, and shared many social events, but I had the distinct feeling that we had never created any activities that would increase deeper understanding across the many cultures that were represented in the class. In particular, I noticed that the kinds of exercises that were typically suggested for learning about another culture were always Level One activities designed to reveal how different cultures manage their daily routines and what one has to avoid in order not to offend someone from another culture. I decided to do an experiment one evening on getting more personal.

I announced to the whole class on Friday that on the

next Tuesday evening I would hold a special class on cross-cultural acquaintanceship for anyone interested in trying something different. About thirty Sloans showed up. I told them that we would do something deeper that night and that they should be prepared to try something new. My purpose was to build a climate in which people were forewarned but curious. I then proceeded as follows:

Ed S.: *For the next half hour you will be working in pairs. We will then debrief and get into a different set of pairs. I want each pair to be two people from different cultures, and I want you to ask each other the questions that really puzzle you about the other culture. I know you already know each other pretty well from being here for a year and doing lots of things together, but I suspect that there are things that you would like to know about each other that you have not dared to ask because it might offend the other person.*

The point of tonight's experiment is to give each other permission to ask those questions and to reveal to each other some of the aspects of your culture that you have not had a chance to talk about. Let's try this for the next half hour. Get yourselves into pairs and try this out."

Sloan: *Should this be about our class behavior or personal stuff or about back-home stuff?*

Ed S.: *It can be about any of those things. What I am doing is giving you permission to ask about something that you want to know, that you are curious about but have never felt you had the right to ask that question because it might be offensive or too personal. I am giving you permission and encouraging you to get more personal even though that is risky.*

(The group then divided into pairs and started their conversations. I noticed that all the pairs were in intense conversations that were actually hard to break up after thirty minutes.)

Ed S.: *How did that go, and do you want to now try it with another pair?*

Sloan 1: *We thought it was very enlightening and would like to continue in our pair if that is okay.*

Sloan 2: *We also thought it was good but would like to now try a different pair.*

Sloan 3: *Several of us would like to be a bigger group and ask some questions of John. In our pair, he was very willing to share his experiences coming from an Alabama sharecropper family and making it into corporate life as a successful manager. Could we meet as a larger group?*

Ed S.: *You are clearly having different experiences, and different needs were revealed, so for the next hour, I think it would be fine if you individually decided how you want to proceed. I will roam around the room and see if anyone needs guidance.*

(For the next hour the groups composed and recomposed themselves spontaneously and asked one another a variety of questions. Five people congregated around John, the African American who had volunteered to tell his story. I again noticed the emotional intensity in the room. At the end of the hour, I brought everyone together to debrief the whole session and got a uniformly positive response along the lines of "I wish we had done some of this sooner." The group that met with John was especially grateful, as was he, that they had been able to get to know him at a deeper level and learn that he was actually quite anxious to tell his fellow students his story.)

LESSONS

- To me the most striking thing was that a multicultural group that officially "knew one another well and had shared many experiences together" was still only functioning at what amounted to a multicultural Level One. They knew one another in their roles as students and social friends, but they had never given themselves permission to personalize across the cultural boundary. Some individual pairs had broken through this during the year and had become friends in a broader sense, often through shared parenting experiences or trips together. But even frequent meals together had not broken some of the barriers around "Don't get too personal, you might offend."

- If personalization is desired across hierarchical, occupational, or cultural boundaries, there has to be a mechanism to make it safe—what I call a "cultural island" on which either the authority gives permission to violate some of the cultural rules or the group creates that climate for itself (Schein, 2010). As the next case shows, organizations sometimes create special events to try to facilitate this.

CASE 10. Levels of Involvement with Ciba-Geigy

My five years of involvement with Ciba-Geigy (C-G), a chemical and pharmaceutical company based in Basel, Switzerland, taught me a great deal about how the helping process has to be varied in terms of the cultural norms of the client system. I ended up with a mix of some rigid Level One relationships because I was the Herr Professor Doctor expert from MIT, and some Level Two relationships that were deliberately encouraged by the CEO and some of his subordinates.

PERSONALIZATION WITH THE CEO

I had just arrived at the Zurich airport after a very glamorous first-class flight from Boston, which included a sumptuous dinner served from a cart, a couple of hours of sleep, and an equally fancy breakfast. I was met by my host, Dr. Jurg Leupold, head of Management Development. He had heard me speak at a 1977 meeting about my research on career anchors, which showed that even people in the same occupation have different self-concepts of why they are in that career (Schein and Van Maanen, 2014), and had decided to recruit me to address the next annual meeting of C-G's worldwide executives.

We had several cordial Level One telephone conversations leading up to the invitation to meet their group chair and CEO, Sam Koechlin, to get acquainted and to "test the chemistry" between us. Leupold explained to me that Koechlin was from an old Basel family and had thoroughly Swiss-German roots but had spent much of his recent career in the US subsidiary and acquired many American values. One of those values was to bring new ideas to his senior management.

I was driven directly to the Koechlins' country house outside of Basel and was welcomed as Dr. Koechlin's guest to spend the day and next night with him and his family. I met Mrs. Koechlin, had dinner with the whole family, and spent many hours with Dr. Koechlin talking about his need to show his executive group that more innovation and creativity was not only necessary for the company's survival but was something that all executives were capable of. He feared that only his scientists or entrepreneurs thought they could be creative, so when he learned about career anchors, he noted immediately that in every anchor category it was possible to be a role innovator. He wanted my lecture to emphasize that all managers in all functions had the power and capacity to create and innovate.

Koechlin and his planning task force also wanted to introduce in lecture format the other exercise in the career anchor booklet—job/role planning. This exercise asks the job occupant to identify all the persons who have expectations of how the occupant in the role should be doing his job, and then to analyze for himself where there are role ambiguities and possible conflicts. Koechlin told me he planned to ask the top three levels of management to do such an analysis during the year after the meeting, as well as having them invite their subordinates to do the career anchor exercise as a basis for the annual career development discussion.

To facilitate all of this, a German-speaking American manager would be assigned to translate the career anchor booklet so that it could be read ahead of the meeting by those managers who were not fluent in English. I would give the lecture and then have the participants, including top executives and even the external board chair, pair up and actually do the anchor interview so that they would learn what their own anchor was.

The chemistry between us was good, so I was signed up for that year's annual meeting, to be followed by two-day quarterly follow-up meetings in Basel. I was driven back to the airport and flown home, first-class, to await the summer meeting four months hence.

LESSONS

■ The impact on me as a consultant was powerful. Not only to be flown over first-class but then to be included in the CEO's personal life was unique. It provided the opportunity for a genuine Level Two relationship to form, enabling me to get a real sense of what Koechlin was actually after in this project. I was surprised and definitely pleased at the degree to which he wanted to incorporate my ideas and the accompanying exercises into his organization's regular working process.

■ The contrast between Ken Olsen introducing me to DEC by lecturing me and then plunging me into his group, and Sam Koechlin inviting me for an overnight and then planning to have me present to his group and do a planned exercise with my materials was striking, and it was a great introduction to thinking about organizational cultures. Not only were the companies completely different, but I also learned that the stiff formality of the Swiss that I had encountered in Dr. Leupold did not preclude them from going almost to the other extreme in the invitation to stay overnight with the Koechlins. It alerted me to the fact that the rules of when and how to get personal can be decidedly different in different national cultures.

LEVEL ONE FORMAL PREPARATION FOR THE SUMMER MEETING

I had a few months back at MIT before it was time to go to the summer annual meeting at Merligen, a resort on Lake Thun in Switzerland. During that time I first was visited by the C-G manager who was translating my booklet, and I learned a bit more about the company. He was a senior manager from the US subsidiary, which, I learned, produced one-third of C-G's annual revenue. He also warned me that I would be receiving a formal visit from Mr. Kunz, the manager who planned, organized, and ran the three-day annual meeting.

Mr. Kunz was very formal, very demanding, and very precise. I was to prepare my lecture in writing so that it could be translated and distributed when I gave my talk. The official language of C-G was English, but not all participants were fluent in it. I was also to prepare my transparencies a month in advance so that they could be translated. I was briefed about the meeting mechanics and told I could stay for the three days and participate in the other activities, which would include some recreational time as well on the third day. Precisely what we were to do was held highly secret from everyone so that we could all enjoy the surprise.

LESSONS

- I had been used to working as a process consultant, so this onslaught of formality and putting me so squarely in the expert role took me by surprise and made me uncomfortable in being so totally different from Koechlin's more personal informal approach. I had given lectures but had never before been made responsible for managing a whole afternoon with formal exercises at an international meeting of the senior executives of a major corporation. In previous work I had learned to be more reactive and to improvise. On this occasion I had no latitude around my participation because, from their point of view, careful planning and crisp execution was the way to get things done. I was not about to be allowed to change that, but I remember saying to myself that I hoped things would loosen up during the meeting so that I could help in ways other than lecturing.

LEVEL ONE HELP DURING THE FIRST ANNUAL MEETING

I was received in Merligen as the outside expert professor
from MIT, treated with an inordinate amount of respect,
and expected to know everything about all aspects of
personnel, labor relations, and career development around
the world. I did not realize it at the time, but expecting me
to know everything pertaining to my field was a reflection of an important assumption within the C-G culture: a
manager should be *totally* on top of his job, and a professor
should know everything in his field.

The lecture, pairing up, and conducting of the mutual
interviews went well, with all participants engaged, even
the chair of the board. Much of the meeting was devoted
to career anchors and job/role planning discussions, with
Koechlin giving the orders that not only the fifty or so top
executives at the meeting but also their subordinates were
to do the job/role analysis on their own jobs and arrange
to have the next echelon under them do it as well. They
were encouraged to ask their subordinates to do the career
anchors, which would provide shared concepts and a
common vocabulary for the annual career development
discussions.

I got to know many of the executives over meals and
learned more about C-G by attending the other activities,
which were mostly progress reports by the major country groups. The surprise event on the last afternoon and
evening was crossbow shooting, an activity that had been
planned to reduce us all to the same level of incompetence
and that, I discovered, was their deliberate plan to personalize relationships in the group. After we had all finished
laughing at one another's incompetence, we were all taken
to a special "Tom Jones dinner," where we ate medieval
style with our hands and were thereby further reduced to

equal status. Informal speeches were made, the chair of the board joked about his own career anchor, and with much beer and wine we all fell into jolly camaraderie.

All in all, this turned out to be an incredible ego-boosting activity, both from the point of view of having my work adopted but also from learning that I could work as an expert with a group like this. Koechlin confirmed that he wanted me to visit quarterly, to work with Dr. Leupold on future career development issues, to get to know more of the internal board members, and to plan to come to next year's annual meeting. During my quarterly visits, I would meet various members of the internal board, which, in effect, operated as a kind of group CEO. They were cordial, remarkably friendly, and excellent hosts, but the only form of help they sought was opinions or information about things that they expected to be within my area of expertise.

LESSONS

- I learned that the meaning of personalizing varies by culture. I clearly had developed a Level Two relationship with Koechlin in that I could ask him how he felt things were going and whether he was achieving some of his goals. He, in turn, was able to share with me some of his worries about the state of denial of many of the executives about the future of the organization if they did not become both more innovative and more conscious of the importance of productivity.

- I learned that if you are locked into an expert role, it is not easy to personalize, because both personal revelations and personal questions are viewed immediately as inappropriate. Even when we were informally playing and eating together, I felt that professional distance had to be

maintained. We could laugh and play together, but I had
a clear sense that even among themselves they carefully
maintained Level One relationships.

HELPING WITH MAJOR RESTRUCTURING AT THE SECOND ANNUAL MEETING

I returned to the second summer meeting to reinforce the
career anchor and job/role planning, but it turned out that
I was needed in a different expert role at the second annual
meeting. Koechlin and the internal board had decided that
a major restructuring was in order, which would include
sharply cutting back the chemical sectors, strengthening
the pharmaceutical sector, and commencing a variety of
cost-related personnel actions, including some extensive
layoffs in all the subsidiary companies.

The internal board believed that the senior executives
did not appreciate the gravity of C-G's financial situation,
so they hired one of the external board members, who was
a professor at the Harvard Business School, to come to this
meeting to convince them that they had a crisis and had to
launch a major change program. After this professor had
convinced the group that they were facing a financial crisis
and had to do a major downsizing and reorganization, I
was asked to provide them with a process model of the
change process that would enable them to begin to figure
out the next steps they could take.

After my lecture on change, I divided the group into
small problem-solving teams to learn how to set change
targets and do force-field analyses of what would be
involved in working toward those targets. We reviewed the
group reports, and I consolidated their change thinking
with a review of the model. I drew heavily on my elabora-
tion of the Lewin change model that I had originally devel-

oped in my analysis of personal, group, and organizational changes (Schein and Bennis, 1965; Schein, 2010) and had used successfully in culture change projects. My expertise here was to provide them with a workable set of steps for (1) analyzing the forces favoring and resisting the desired change; (2) thinking about change as adaptive moves; (3) setting change goals; (4) organizing those goals into focused projects to implement change; and, most of all, (5) developing some confidence that change was actually possible.

Many good ideas came out, which, when shared, reassured the executive group that the restructuring was feasible. The regional groups did, however, note that the Basel headquarters was grossly overstaffed and that it too would have to cut back drastically. The internal board took all the suggestions from the groups and organized them into twenty-five projects, each of which would be driven by a board member and a handpicked task force of executives.

At my quarterly visits, I was to help the internal board with the management of these task forces. In effect, I had succeeded in becoming a process expert and coach, helping with here-and-now individual and group problems. I was also available to individual task force leaders to provide whatever coaching help they felt they needed, which usually meant a couple of hours of conversation where my main role was to reflect, to restructure, and to make occasional suggestions on the management of the project groups.

During these visits other aspects of the organizational culture surfaced and reinforced the deep assumptions that the only kind of acceptable help was expert information from an outside expert or the boss. Just asking for help was considered not being on top of one's job, which was shown most dramatically when I would pass someone with whom

I had just spent a couple of hours discussing ways he could run his task force, would nod to say hello, and would find the person staring past me as if he did not know me. Dr. Leupold explained that talking to the outside consultant could be construed among their peers as a sign of weakness that they did not want to display!

A related incident revealed another aspect of this cultural element. I had talked to a lot of managers about their downsizing approaches and learned that the successful managers always delivered the message personally and supplemented it with helpful offers of support. I wrote this up as a "Memo on Downsizing" and asked Dr. Leupold to distribute it to other managers who might need it. One day when I was counseling a manager during a quarterly visit, the following conversation took place.

Mgr.: *Welcome, Professor Schein. As you know we have to release a lot of people. I wonder what advice you might give me as to how best to do this?*

Ed S.: *Have you seen my memorandum on what I found to be some common useful approaches for downsizing? Many of these were based on what I learned from other C-G managers.*

Mgr.: *No, I have not.*

Ed S.: *I left it with Dr. Leupold on my last quarterly visit.*

Mgr.: *Let me call his office right now and ask about it.*

(He calls his secretary.)

Mgr.: *Frau Beck, please call Dr. Leupold's office and ask about the Schein memo on downsizing.*

(A few minutes later, she comes back.)

Secr.: *Yes, I called, and they said they had it and would be
happy to send it over by messenger right away.*

(We continue our talk, and within ten minutes a messenger arrives with a copy of my memo. I wondered
why it had not been sent to this project manager
before.)

Other managers with whom I talked also had not seen
my memo, which made me wonder why my memo had not
been distributed. I was having dinner with one of C-G's
internal organizational consultants and asked him about
this. He immediately concurred that he had had similar
experiences with developing a training program for a manager in one department and discovering that even though
it was highly successful, other managers did not seem to
know about it. Why did information not flow more easily
across hierarchical and even peer group boundaries?

My colleague analyzed it as being the result of a particular norm that he saw operating in the company: "My job is
my personal empire; I am completely in charge of it and do
not need unsolicited help. To give me unsolicited advice on
how to do my job is comparable to walking into my home
uninvited!"

I then realized that when I said to Dr. Leupold "distribute
this memo," I was asking him to do something that was not
culturally possible in C-G. I was asking him to risk offending various managers by giving them my memo when they
had not asked for it. When they asked, he sent it immediately by messenger!

My colleague and I then deciphered a whole other set of
cultural artifacts that led to the conclusion that this sense
of ownership of one's job and building walls around it had
two major consequences: (1) Managers made it a point to

be on top of their jobs and to be very well informed. And (2) information about innovations, guidelines, checklists, and other bits and pieces of "help" did not circulate. Only if top management forced something down through the system would information of this sort reach everyone. The irony in this discovery is that, had I known of this norm, I could have gotten a list of addresses from Leupold of people who he thought might benefit and sent them the memo from MIT. I would then have found managers to be extremely grateful for the help because, after all, I was the hired expert, so this gave them some sense of getting their money's worth. They could accept some advice from me, but my memo coming from Leupold would make them feel that Leupold was seeing them as needing help, which they could not admit. Culture works so unconsciously that Leupold was not aware of this whole process. He assumed that "distribute it" meant to have it available in case any manager wanted it.

At the end of the second annual meeting, we again had a fun outing, this time a sport called "Hornussen," in which you must hit an iron ball down a driving range with a short rigid stick to which is attached a two-foot leather thong at the end of which is the hard driving piece. Even making contact with the ball at all was nearly impossible.

LESSONS

■ I learned a great deal about how dominant, constraining, and awkward Level One professional relations can be. Level One relations made it easy to give advice, but I never felt I learned what problems or issues were really on managers' minds and therefore whether the advice was helpful or not.

■ I also learned that some of the subtle elements of culture
   cannot be deciphered by the outsider, even with a lot of
   observation. Until I asked some questions of Dr. Leupold,
   and later my organization development (OD) colleague,
   I simply did not understand some of the behavior I was
   observing. As ethnographers have learned, one needs
   insider informants to really understand culture.

THE THIRD ANNUAL MEETING AND THE CULTURE LECTURE DISASTER

At the end of the second visit, Koechlin asked me to under-
take a more formal study of the C-G culture, because of his
conviction that it would help the group to become more
conscious of its own culture as they implemented their
change projects. This was a special project that completely
content-seduced me because organizational culture was
becoming my main research interest. Koechlin was giving
me a gift: to study his organization, report the data in the
1981 annual meeting, and draw out the implications for the
change projects. What an opportunity, and, as it turned out,
what a trap!

I developed a pretty good picture of the key assumptions
that were driving C-G and could see how they were related
to the history of the company and the Swiss-German
culture (Schein, 2010). Much of the formality and careful
planning clearly was connected, first, to the constraints
of working with chemicals and biological products, and,
second, to the formality of the national culture, which was
reinforced by the discipline that all C-G managers learned
when they spent their compulsory time in the Swiss army.
Driving all of this was their self-image of an important
company doing valuable things for the world's benefit. I
presented my analysis with many concrete examples and

saw many heads nodding, but I did not anticipate that there were others in the audience, some of them senior executives on the internal board, who were quite offended about several points, especially my seeing a connection to the Swiss army.

During the Q&A one of them said: "Professor Schein, you have it all wrong; you do not understand the army or the C-G culture at all!" As others entered into the discussion, some agreeing with the comment and some disagreeing, it polarized the group and led eventually to recommendations by some board members that my future consulting should be limited to working just with the Management Development group. For some key people, I had clearly failed in my expert role, and unfortunately the polarization within the executive group prevented any further serious discussion of what the relevant cultural themes were that needed to be considered in relation to the change projects.

I was later able to salvage my "expert on process" role a bit with the steering committee of the worldwide change program. That committee included some members of the internal board who felt I had gotten it right and wanted continuing help on the management of the twenty-five or so major change projects that were underway.

In the meantime Koechlin had become ill and withdrew from active management, which left the internal board without a strong leader. The person who took over was not one of the old Swiss scientists and was one of the people who agreed with my culture analysis. He proposed and sold the idea to his colleagues that I continue on in various capacities. The headquarters downsizing was proceeding with a vengeance and caught Dr. Leupold in its net. However, another cultural element of C-G was to be tremendously caring and supportive of its people, so it tried to ease people out gradually. This combination of circumstances led them to propose that Leupold stay on as a consultant to study the impact of early overseas assignments on the career development of senior executives. They had lots of statistical and historical data for him to analyze. My role as a consultant would be "scientific advisor" to this project "to ensure that the research met formal scientific criteria," and to work informally in a process role with Leupold's successor, Joe Wells, who became head of Management Development. Wells was a much less formal Canadian, which led over the next several years to my having a much more personal Level Two relationship with him.

LESSONS

- Working with C-G as mostly a "content expert" was accepted, but with the culture lecture, I had slipped into the "doctor" role and was giving a diagnosis of their organization. This was a different kind of intervention from what they were used to and led to quite different responses from different members of the organization. I resolved that, in the future whenever culture was involved, I would help the insiders diagnose themselves but would not again fall into the trap of telling a client organization about its own culture.

- Several years later this dilemma came up again when the US subsidiary of C-G asked me to give "the Basel lecture" to the US group to enable them "to see more clearly what went on in Basel where most of my data had been gathered." The US group was curious how my description would fit their own sense of themselves, which led to a shocking conclusion. After I had presented the analysis, they said, "My God, you have just described us perfectly."

They had not realized how strongly the C-G corporate culture had taken over the US subsidiary as well.

■ Working in the Swiss-German culture and in a company based on chemistry strongly highlighted how different companies can be. I could see clearly the impact of: (1) national culture; (2) the impact of chemistry in how work was defined; (3) the risks involved in this industry; (4) the impact of company history and the Basel aristocracy; and, (5) the merger they had undergone. I could not have found a more extreme contrast than when I was simultaneously working with C-G and DEC, a highly successful US start-up computer company.

■ This contrast showed up most clearly in how my role played out. DEC was aggressively determined to solve its own problems and needed me most as a stimulus, catalyst, supporter, and go-between. I steered and stimulated process changes. In C-G I was a career development expert, professor, lecturer, and dispenser of various kinds of wisdom. They expected me to stay in this role and were quite ready to drop me as a consultant if they found my expertise wanting. However, I also learned that when I acted as a Humble Consultant in the various group meetings and in individual coaching sessions with senior executives, they found that role even more helpful, though they did not realize that I was playing a different role at those times.

CASE 11. The Executive Coaching Dilemma—Who Is the Client?

Much of my work with C-G and with DEC involved coaching individuals in their organizational roles. They were individual clients, but I was helping them on behalf of an organizational agenda that was shared by higher levels. However, there were times when I felt that what was best for the organization was not necessarily best for the person I was coaching. It was not always easy to find an adaptive move that could be made by the client that would work out for both him or her and the larger organizational project. This potential conflict arises often when *executive coaching* is involved.

I was supervising an executive coach, Joan, with whom I had already formed a Level Two relationship in prior joint work. She wanted my help to think through her dilemmas in a case where the organization had hired her to coach a senior executive. The client to be coached, Mark, was a high-potential executive who was viewed by his boss as consistently underperforming, seeming to be not really dedicated to the organization's mission and tasks, and spending a lot of time at home.

Joan was told by Mark's boss that Mark had been told that he was viewed as underperforming, that he did not seem to be committed, and that he was spending too much time at home. She was hired by HR on behalf of this boss to coach Mark to become more engaged and to demon-strate more commitment to his job. Joan was given all the performance data about Mark, had had several meetings with him, and now faced a dilemma. Our conversation began with her recounting how she had handled the first meeting.

Joan: *Mark, as you know, I have been asked to coach you. How do you see the issue? Why has your boss asked you to have some coaching?*

(Notice that this is a mixture of humble inquiry and diagnostic inquiry.)

Mark: *Well, my boss seems to think that I am not really committed to what we are doing here, but frankly I don't get it. I feel very committed.*

> (Joan had also been told by the boss that Mark did not seem to realize that being present and working extra hard is one way to show commitment. Joan reported that she could have stayed in humble inquiry and just let Mark continue, but she chose instead to speed up the personalization process by probing the "too much time at home" issue.)

Joan: *Tell me a little bit about yourself, your home life. Are you married, do you have kids?*

Mark: *Sure, well, I am happily married with two kids in high school. My wife has a great job that keeps her very busy and on the road a lot, so some of the time with kids falls to me. We decided a long time ago that we would not bring in nannies or babysitters if it can be avoided, so I get some of the home duty. But let me tell you, I love my job and am very committed to it, and I get everything done on time, so I am not sure why I am perceived as not dedicated.*

> (Joan was inviting an exploration of home life in order to get a sense of why Mark was absent so much. She could have continued to inquire, but she chose to personalize further by revealing something about herself.)

Joan: *I really understand your situation. I have been there myself with a partner who had a tough schedule, and have found my personal and work life got in the way of each other. My partner didn't like all the time I was putting in on work, so I had to decide how to work out my schedule differently. Can you tell me a bit more about how you allocate your time and how you decide how to divide time between work and home?*

(This approach might be called "rapid coaching" in that Joan was not exploring much about Mark's personality or history but was going directly at one of the main symptoms of why he was being coached—too much time away from work.)

Mark: *Let me tell you a bit about my wife. She is from Costa Rica, from a large Catholic family, and they always took family duties to be the most important thing. If there is a birthday or our daughter is in a play or our son is doing some sports thing, we have always committed to being there for them. If I have to be away from the office to see him play, I usually make sure that I am completely caught up on my work and tell my boss where I am going and why. I have assumed that she understood my priorities.*

Joan: *So your wife has strong family loyalties, and I gather you do as well.*

Mark: *Well, I don't feel as strongly as she does with her background, but since she travels, I try to honor her values and do the home duties when I can.*

Joan: *How does your wife deal with her absence from some of the kids' activities?*

(This was a circular question to learn more about the wife's situation.)

Mark: *Well, it bothers her a lot, but she feels that if at least one parent is there, between us, we are meeting her values.*

(In this reported interview, I was, of course, aware that Joan might be skipping steps, but I was observing that with each of Mark's responses, Joan was testing the relationship in order to determine when she could become even more suggestive. When she believed that

they trusted each other and had a Level Two relationship building, she tried a more direct suggestion to
determine whether Mark had been too passive in
accepting the home duties and what it might take to get
him to be more active in claiming time for the office.)

Joan: *Have you considered telling your wife that you might be
required to spend more time at your job in the future?*

(Note that the feedback that Mark has been spending
too little time at the office was put in a *future* context
to avoid getting into a defensive denial from Mark that
he was not spending enough time based on getting his
work done.)

Mark: *I don't see the need to do that since I have enough time
now to get all my work done and could do even more, so why
would that change? . . .*

(The coach then faced the basic choice point: whether
to pursue the *company's need* to change Mark or to
pursue *Mark's need* to continue to be successful at
the low level of presence that he is exhibiting, even
though that might mean the end of his career in that
company. If her change target became to get Mark to
commit more to the company by renegotiating time
commitments with his wife, her coaching was more
akin to indoctrination, trying to get the client to fit into
the company. If she chose to help Mark sort out his
life in general by accepting his current time allocation,
she became more of an independent career counselor.
Joan then reported a further complication when Mark
challenged the process.)

Mark: *One thing you should understand is that my boss is
very confused about this time thing anyway. She has never*

asked me to keep specific hours, always emphasizing just getting the job done. There are others in the office who are away more than I am, so I consider her demands of me completely unfair, since I get my job done. I don't know why I am supposed to see a coach.

Joan: *So you are feeling that even this coaching is unfair.*

Mark: *Absolutely. I could tell you other things about my boss, her favoritism, and her poor communication. Like I said, she has never said to me, "Mark, I expect you at the office nine to five," so I don't really know why we are meeting or what I am doing wrong.*

When Joan reported this, we switched into a joint analysis and pondered whether she should force the issue by asking Mark the following: *If your boss were clear about this, if she told you, as she told me in briefing me about this, that your time away from the office is a problem because it makes you seem uncommitted, how might you go about dealing with that request?*

We agreed that Mark's answer to this question would determine the direction of the coaching, whether to try to change Mark to meet the company's needs or help him to decide whether he should pursue his future elsewhere. But Joan now had the additional dilemma of wondering how accurate Mark's perception of his boss was. It suddenly was not clear who was the client, on whose behalf Joan was supposed to work. The company was paying Joan, but that did not automatically mean that she had to honor what Mark's boss or HR wanted. Maybe the boss needed coaching more than Mark? Joan had to consider whether the whole organization as client would benefit more by "fixing" Mark, helping Mark out of the company, and/or confronting Mark's boss with the lack of clarity in her communications to Mark. This had suddenly become one of those complex, messy problems for which there is no solution, only several possible adaptive moves.

When Joan and I next talked, she reported that she did ask Mark whether he understood that his absences were viewed as lack of commitment and learned that he was adamant about his view that if he got his work done he should be entitled to go home. She decided to help Mark with his version of his problem, which eventually led to his seeking a different job. She decided not to confront Mark's boss. For herself she decided that to be an executive coach being paid by the company to "fix" someone was too much like indoctrination, and she could not see herself being really helpful in that situation, so she ceased to take on such coaching jobs unless the company explicitly licensed her to work primarily with the client's needs.

LESSONS

■ The most important lesson of this case is that had Joan not personalized the conversation, it would never have come out what was really going on, either with Mark or with Mark's boss. By revealing her own version of Mark's dilemma, she found out about Mark's family values that clearly influenced the situation. Most important of all, she finally was trusted enough for Mark to tell her his view of his boss and how he thought the whole process was unfair.

■ The second lesson is that Joan's dilemma did not have an easy answer. She was caught in an organizational tangle where perceptions by the different actors did not add up, which made it hard to see possible courses of action clearly. She had to rely to some extent on her own values to decide whether to further explore the complex situation between Mark and his boss, which might ultimately help the company, or whether to help Mark resolve his dilemma, potentially at the company's expense.

■ The third lesson is that the question of who is the client can become very complicated, and the helper often ends up in a situation where the needs of different parts of the client system require different kinds of responses from the helper. Had Joan gone back to the boss to inquire further what was going on, they might well have uncovered a whole series of new issues between that boss and others in the organization, issues that might not have been solvable by Joan.

CASE 12. An Unfortunate Personalization Mistake

I was asked by the head of manufacturing of a local high-tech company to sit in on the meetings of the manufacturing committee to see if I could be helpful in making the committee more productive. I sat in on the meetings and would either intervene directly if I thought it would help or coach the head of manufacturing after the meeting on what he could have done to make the meeting more effective. I viewed my client to be primarily the committee and secondarily the head of manufacturing, and, in retrospect, I see that I entered the group in a self-appointed expert role.

After watching several meetings, I observed one member being very quiet, contributing occasionally but then being pretty much ignored when he did come in with a comment. This seemed unfair to me and provided a great opportunity to point out to the group how they might be more effective if participation levels were more equal. I waited for an opportunity when he spoke, and was as usual ignored, to point out to the group what had just happened. An embarrassed silence fell over the group, the chair gave me perfunctory thanks, and he went on with the next agenda item.

After the meeting the chair pulled me aside and explained that Joe, the ignored member, had been one of the great technical contributors in the history of the company but had had a mild stroke and was now not only less able to contribute but was also very much in need of a job and was still much loved in the company. The management examined their options of what to do with Joe, and decided to "park" him with the manufacturing committee, where people still appreciated him even though his ideas were now quite obsolete. They had observed that Joe seemed glad to have a role, a job, and a place to be and that he did not seem to mind that his ideas were rarely picked up. What my intervention had done was to embarrass Joe and the rest of the group because they could not explain their behavior without further embarrassment.

LESSONS

■ Innocent questions that point to a particular person can be extremely powerful personalizing interventions, but they can also be powerfully disruptive if they expose unseen forces in the group. My intervention forced an issue into the open that the group had long ago laid to rest. My motivation was to bring Joe into the group, to personalize his relationship to the group, but all I had accomplished was probably to make his role even more marginal. Joe and the group did not have areas of interdependence, so the Level One relationship between Joe and the group was working perfectly well.

- Don't get ahead of your client with your own agenda. I should have asked the chair after one of the meetings why Joe was so consistently ignored; I then would not have been bothered by what I observed.

- Don't assume that more personalization is always better. Many relationships work very well at Level One when there are no interdependencies.

Summary and Conclusions

In Chapter 4, I focused on how personalization begins in the very first interaction. In this chapter I have analyzed the interpersonal and cultural issues that are involved in personalization, and by implication I have raised the question of when it is desirable for either consultant or client to engage in further deepening of the relationship. The cases illustrate that reaching the Level Two relationship through personalization is not always necessary, but the more complex the problem is and the more it involves interdependencies, the more important Level Two interaction becomes.

I have also argued that you need to get to this Level Two relationship in order to determine *how* to help, and you may well discover that the client needs a specific kind of expert or doctor, which means that you cannot help. If you don't personalize to *some* degree and build *some* Level Two trust, you will not know whether or not you are working the right problem and whether your help will really be helpful. It sounds paradoxical, and it is because it requires perpetual here-and-now diagnosis of the situation into which you are thrust.

What the cases also illustrate is that in a complex organizational situation the consultant often finds that she is working with multiple clients, some of whom require humble consulting while others want only expert help. Such expert help was often needed around the processes that clients wanted to pursue, leading to many situations where the humble consultant had to find adaptive moves that involved doing something different than what the client may have had in mind. We turn in the next chapter to a more detailed analysis of those kinds of process moves.

SUGGESTION FOR THE READER

Get together with one or two colleagues and ask yourselves the following question: "If we are trying to help someone, such as when we coach him or her, what are some specific ways we can convey the desire to be more personal without overstepping into intimacy?" Be specific and give examples. The goal is to explore in a creative way what is appropriate personalization and what is pushing the boundary too far.

SIX

The Humble Consulting Focus on Process

Probably the most important rule of thumb for keeping a constructive Level Two helping relationship alive is to *avoid content seduction.* The odds of the outside helper being able to come up with a workable helpful content suggestion is, in my view, extremely small. The important point is to not confuse empathy with content seduction. Empathy is understanding the client's situation, and maybe even being sympathetic to it, but never forgetting for a minute that you are not in the client's shoes and therefore cannot possibly figure out what to do that might work in his culture. On the other hand, once you have a sense of what the client is after, you and the client can explore adaptive moves *together* and, in that context, you can make *process* suggestions that occur to you that might help.

This raises an important question: are you, the humble consultant, bringing anything else to the relationship beyond commitment, curiosity, and caring? In my experience the likely answer is that you may have more experience of, and sense about, interpersonal, group, and organizational processes. The humble consultant's training and experience will be most valuable in helping the client consider the possible consequences of different kinds of adaptive moves. If you have been trained in organization development, management consulting, or coaching, you will have encountered many examples of the different ways that things can be thought about and can be done. Sometimes the client is stuck precisely on this point—she knows what goal she is trying to achieve but does not have a good sense of how to get there, or even how to begin.

Cases of Problem Restructuring

CASE 13. A Question That Restructured Alcoa Australia

I had been asked to do a workshop on career anchors with a group of managers in the headquarters of Alcoa Australia and was having lunch after the workshop with the CEO and his executive team. The CEO had been a Sloan Fellow at MIT, so I already had a Level Two working relationship with him. The story begins in the middle of lunch.

CEO: *Ed, would you mind if we did a bit of business over lunch?*

Ed S.: *Of course not, just go ahead.*

CEO to his team at the table: *You all know that Paul, our VP of Administration is retiring, so we should be ready with a replacement appointment. Could we talk about that for a minute? What do you all think of Steve as his replacement?*

VP of Finance: *Steve is a good man, but somehow I don't feel quite comfortable having him in the VP of Admin job. I am not sure why.*

CEO: *He is our best candidate, is he not?*

VP of Operations: *Yes he is, but I also have some hesitation. I cannot put my finger on the issue, though.*

CEO: *What do you think, Al? You relate to a lot of those functions.*

Al: *I think Steve is great; we should give him the job, but I wonder why some of us are hesitating. I too have a bit of hesitation.*

> (At this point I got really curious about their inability to resolve this issue and wondered to myself what might be the issue with Steve, but the group seemed not to be able to talk about him in specifics. Instead, I chose an "innocent" analytical question that I was curious about.)

Ed S.: *Sorry for jumping into the conversation, but I am curious what the VP of Administration does. What is that job?*

CEO (in a patient and patronizing tone): *Well, Ed, he heads a bunch of functions, all the parts of Human Resources and Personnel, all the internal accounting and finance functions, public relations . . .*

Al (jumping in and interrupting the CEO): *That's exactly where I have my problem. Steve is a great administrator, but I don't see him able to handle public relations.*

VP of Operations: *I think you nailed it, Al. I think the world of Steve, but he never has been good outside with the press and all.*

VP of Finance: *I agree; I can see Steve in all the functions except PR.*

Al: *That raises an interesting point: does PR have to be part of the VP of Admin job? In fact, as I think about it, our PR problems with the environmentalists are growing; our mining operations in Pinjara are running into new government policies concerning aboriginal land claims. I think maybe we should have a new and separate VP of Environmental Affairs and PR.*

CEO: *Interesting idea, could work. What do you all think?*

VP of Finance: *I think it would solve our problem. Give Steve the functions where we all think he is great, move PR to this new expanded concept, and hire someone in whom we can have complete confidence.*

All agreed, and we went back to informal talk.

LESSONS

- I don't think they realized that my innocent question had led to a problem solution. What I learned yet again is that help can come in brief, innocent interventions that help clients to approach dilemmas from a new angle. The group had only one process for working on the problem: to analyze Steve and his strengths or weaknesses, but they could not even do that because analytically they had no tools for thinking about the different skills of an executive. My question had shifted the process of problem solving away from the person to the job to be done, and, as it turned out, that gave them the analytical vehicle for discussing what they did and did not like about Steve's qualifications. I had shifted the problem-solving **process,** which then enabled the group to move forward to resolution.

CASE 14. The Team-Building Retreat in the Quincy Plant of Proctor & Gamble

Procter & Gamble (P&G) was in the middle of a major program of changing the manufacturing processes in all of their plants. I was working as a consultant to Art, the manager of the Quincy plant outside of Boston. My job was to meet with Art and his team from time to time to help him calibrate their skills and to give him feedback on his management style. The team consisted of several functional managers and the Organizational Development (OD) specialist, who was a former union employee who had been sent to learn OD skills and then was returned to the plant from which he had come to help with team and management problems.

Using a former insider to learn OD skills and bringing him back to the plant where he already had relationships was a highly enlightened approach to bringing OD skills into an organization in an organic way, an approach that P&G was using in all their plants as part of the overall productivity improvement program. Art decided to do an off-site team-building retreat and wanted to meet with me and his OD staffer to design the program details. We were meeting at the MIT faculty club over lunch. When it was time to get to work, I asked a simple "dumb question" to facilitate the planning.

Ed S.: *Art, how many people will actually attend the meeting?*

Art: *Well, let me think . . . There will be my main engineer, my HR guy, the quality control manager, purchasing, finance . . . Well, actually I am still ambivalent about my finance guy, he has not proven himself yet . . . I may have to replace him . . .*

(long pause) . . . You know, Ed, now that you make me think about it, I wonder whether we should have the retreat with one guy I am not sure of. Let's postpone the event.

OD mgr.: *I think that would be wise. Building a team with one person who may not make it sounds like a risk to me. We should be able to tell whoever comes to the retreat that "you are my team."*

Art: *Sorry about this, Ed, but let's just put a hold on this.*

Ed S.: *Nothing to be sorry about. Sounds like the right deci-sion until you have your final team in place.*

LESSONS

- I considered this to be a great success, triggered by an innocent but pertinent question of who would be there, an analysis that Art had clearly not done yet needed to do to avoid the mess of building a team, and then firing one member. It reinforced in me how important it is to ask the question to which you do not know the answer and to force a discussion of goals and process at a concrete behavioral level.

CASE 15. Abandoning Building a Team Culture in a Sales Organization

I got a call from the VP of Sales of a large multidivisional company.

VP (on the phone): *Hi, Professor Schein, I wonder if I could come by to discuss some restructuring ideas I have for our sales force. I want to change the culture of the sales force and would appreciate your input. I will be at MIT next week. Could we have lunch?*

Ed S.: *Sounds interesting. I am free on Tuesday or Wednesday.*

(I was extremely curious about what restructuring a sales force and changing its culture could mean, so I was happy to have lunch with him. At the lunch the following conversation took place.)

VP: *Here is the problem as I see it. We have different product lines, each with their own sales force, but they also report to a corporate sales manager who integrates all the marketing and sales. We are getting a lot of customer complaints that salespeople come in from the different divisions with sometimes different incentives, sometimes contradicting each other and sometimes even competing with each other. I want to launch a training program to build a culture of teamwork and collaboration among the salespeople.*

Ed S.: *Can you give me some examples of how the present system works and what you imagine the ideal future system would look like?*

(I was trying to pin down what he meant by a "culture of teamwork" through asking questions that forced concrete behavioral examples. You are influencing the client's *thinking process* when you ask for examples and "force" the client to imagine what the future behavior would look like if the desired change occurs. It is only when that future state is defined behaviorally that you can jointly assess whether the existing culture would enable or block the change.)

VP: *Well, right now each division schedules its sales calls independently, so the individual salespeople don't coordinate their visits to the customer. I would like them to go out as teams and plan their sales pitches together so that the* *customer would get a more unified picture of what we are selling and what kinds of deals or discounts we are willing to make. Right now, different sales groups actually offer deals that contradict each other and sometimes compete in what they are selling the customer.*

Ed S.: *Let me see if I understand this. In the present state, a customer might see salespeople from different divisions at unpredictably different times and might get different stories on what kinds of discounts and deals are being offered by your company?*

VP: *Exactly. We need to teach our salespeople to coordinate more, tell the same story, and visit the customer as teams, not as individuals.*

Ed S.: *Okay, so if sales teams went out together as teams and were successful in selling what the customer really needed because they are now working together, how would you reward them? What is your current reward system, and would that have to change?*

> (This is the critical diagnostic question, because, as you may be aware, most sales forces are paid on an individual incentive system, have quotas, and are rewarded as competing individuals. If the client does not realize what may be involved in the change he desires, you may have to spell it out further.)

VP: *Well, of course, like all sales forces, they are on individual incentives and quotas, but I want them to develop a team attitude and team spirit when they visit clients together.*

Ed S.: *Do you think that is possible given the present reward structure?*

VP: *What do you mean?*

Ed S.: *Would you, for example, institute group rewards and group incentives if they went out as teams and were successful in helping each other solve the customer's real problem? Would you be willing to change the deeper culture of sales from individual to group incentives?*

VP: *I don't really see that happening in this organization. We are deeply committed to individual performance measurement.*

Ed S.: *So within that individualistic culture is there some small change you could make that would reduce the customer complaints?*

> (I am now focusing on the client's real concern—customer complaints—to see if they could be dealt with adaptively without changing the whole reward system of the sales organization.)

VP: *Well, I suppose we could develop a better cross-divisional scheduling system for sales visits and have someone coordinate these visits, or if we find salespeople going to the same customer, have them coordinate their pitch before they meet the customer, . . . or have them meet periodically around given customers to see how they could each benefit from a conversation about that customer.*

Ed S.: *Those all sound like viable options.*

VP: *You are right; that gives me some ideas. Maybe we don't need a training program and a new culture of teamwork and collaboration.*

> (By being forced into a more careful behavioral analysis of what the client's desired "culture change" would entail, the client begins to rethink what might be involved, what is possible, and what is not. He has been forced to think in terms of small adaptive

moves instead of grand culture changes and has been reminded of what is really worrying him.)

LESSONS

■ The biggest lesson I learned is that clients often do not think through what is involved in the changes they desire—what else in the culture would have to change to make their desired change. They tend to think of culture in "local" terms as a separate thing that can be manipulated without consequence to the larger system, and they rarely realize that the present culture is the product of structures and processes that have been successful in the past and are therefore exceedingly stable, that is, the individualistic incentive system.

■ The real problem has to be identified: the customer complaints and how to reduce them. Another small adaptive move might be to go to selected customers and find out in more detail just what it is that they are most bothered by before designing a general fix like "a culture of teamwork." With hindsight I feel I should have asked whether they have talked to customers about exactly what it is that bothers them.

Cases on Changing the Consultant's or Client's Process Solutions

CASE 16. Successfully Reducing Engineering Turnover in the General Electric Lynn Plant

Every now and then a consulting opportunity comes along that is ideal in content and location. Such was the case when the personnel manager of the large General Electric

(GE) plant in Lynn, Massachusetts, asked me to help him with the high turnover of engineers that the plant was experiencing. I followed my principle of asking him to come to MIT to discuss what he had in mind. Over lunch he showed me statistics on how a large percentage of the best new engineers that they hired each year left within two or three years, an unacceptable situation.

Reducing turnover in this population was a pretty clear improvement goal that we could agree on. I concurred in his analysis, how he defined the problem, and his goal of reducing turnover, but I did not agree with his proposal to have me interview a large number of engineers and then recommend what management should do differently.

Clients often think they know *how* they want a problem approached, and because they are paying for it, they think they know what the consultant can and should do for them. He wanted the report with my analysis and recommendations within six months.

Interviewing people, finding out what was wrong and recommending a fix was certainly the traditional approach and would provide good consulting work for me. But I had an intuition that his approach could be improved upon, that there was a better *process* available for achieving the lower turnover goals. The goal, after all, was not my report but to actually reduce turnover. Was there a way to go straight to the final goal?

I suggested that this problem be turned over to a hand-picked task force of engineers who were in the second year of their employment at GE and who were considered to be prototypes of the kind of employees they wanted to keep. Have this task force work with me and be my client. We would jointly decide what data to gather and work out a change strategy to reduce turnover. I would function as their coach, but they would own the problem and be accountable to GE management to solve the problem. GE management would select them, give them some time off to work on the project, and set a timetable for results.

Though I only articulated them later, several important principles of change were involved in this plan. *First*, the consultant did not own the problem, nor did the personnel manager. The problem was with the young engineers who were leaving the company, so why not give young engineers the problem to diagnose and fix? *Second*, presently employed engineers would be in the best position to know what to ask and how to interpret the interview data that would be gathered from current engineers and previous engineers who had left. *Third*, presently employed engineers would have here-and-now data about the climate in the organization that might explain people leaving. *Fourth*, presently employed engineers would know best how to implement change within the plant and how to present their results to management in a culturally acceptable manner. *Fifth*, and perhaps most important point of all, if GE was willing to create this task force of young engineers and give them time off to solve this turnover problem, this in itself would be an important first adaptive move that would signal to the whole engineering organization that management was willing to listen and make changes. The diagnostic process itself would be the first and most visible intervention.

A task force was created, and they met with me in a coaching role to, first, lay out a plan of whom to interview about what, and, second and most important, to consider how the project was itself an intervention that would start some change efforts within the plant. The task force members had to understand that the way in which they did the interviews was in itself an intervention, which would cause the interviewees to think about things that they might not otherwise have thought about and, by virtue of having been selected to be interviewed, might influence how they felt about staying at GE.

The group met with me monthly for about six months and uncovered a number of "hygienic factors" in how the plant was managed that clearly demotivated the engineers and yet could easily be changed. The most important finding was that management was not giving enough freedom to the new engineers to develop their own work plans. They were overmanaged, which ironically became abundantly clear to the members of my task force when they were given some freedom to do this project.

The members of the task force became highly effective change agents and continued to work over the next year or so in implementing a whole series of changes that cured the turnover problem and increased morale. The solutions were not surprising: more challenging work, clearer goals, and more autonomy in how to get the job done.

Had we spent a year or more finding this out, we would have had a tough job of convincing management that this was true and an even tougher job in getting anything changed. By having the task force members uncover these factors themselves, the groundwork was laid for how to make changes, because they had the detailed information that would make managers change their behavior.

LESSONS

- I am constantly surprised at how often consultants grab at problems and own them, when it would be both more efficient and valid to turn the problems back to the organization, take on the role of a humble consultant, and coach the organization members to own both the diagnostic work and the implementation of the proposed interventions. All of the diagnostic work was far better handled by task force members, and that process sent a clear message that management wanted to reduce turnover. I was also impressed with how clever the "insider consultants" were in figuring out what management would listen to and what they would reject. The insiders knew nuances of how the culture in GE worked that enabled them to be more effective in bringing about change.

■ I was struck by how my role had to shift within this whole engagement from humble consultant to process doctor to group coach according to the shifting realities of the situation. The experience highlighted that once the relationship with the client has reached Level Two, it is possible to make these role shifts without creating relationship ambiguities.

■ For myself, I discovered how much more fun it was to coach this insider group rather than to decipher the cultural content myself. I had by now learned over and over again that a culture diagnosis works best when done by insiders in connection with a concrete problem that they are trying to solve.

CASE 17. How to Assess and "Evaluate" Culture in a Sales Organization

A few years ago, I was approached by the local subsidiary of a German pharmaceutical company to provide some help on a "senior promotion problem." Executive management had sorted out what they wanted and how they wanted it done but needed a "culture expert" to implement their plan. I was invited to several of their executive meetings, where this whole issue was discussed and their plan was revealed.

The issue was whether to promote from inside or bring in an outsider as VP of Sales. Their current VP, who had built the sales organization and run it for three decades, was going to retire. There was an internal candidate who seemed okay to everyone, but the retirement provided an opportunity to see "whether the culture of the sales organization was okay or needed some changes." I was to investigate this culture and help to determine whether it should be *preserved* by hiring the insider or *changed* by going outside. I concurred that this was a reasonable question, and they had thought it all through to my satisfaction, but their proposal for *how* to proceed was, from my point of view, a problem.

They had budgeted time and money for me to individually interview all of the hundred or more sales reps in order to identify the sales culture and assess it. I never found out whether the hidden agenda here was that the internal candidate was African American and perhaps they wanted to get a sense of how popular he was before they anointed him and/or whether they wanted to know how his approach and his values meshed with those of the sales reps.

I suggested to them that the individual interview process was the wrong approach if they really wanted to assess the culture. I proposed instead some *group* interviews of diagonal slices that would capture all of the departments and units. Group interviews would provide a quicker and better picture of the culture than individual interviews if the sales reps would open up in front of one another. The planning group and the CEO talked this out with me and concurred with my conclusion that group interviews of the reps would work well and provide better data. It turned out that one of the sources of pride in the sales organization was the high trust level between management and the reps, so openness would not be a problem. However, the members of the executive planning group who were negotiating this with me thought that the top two levels of management should be interviewed individually because they might not open up enough in front of one another. I felt that I had developed a Level Two relationship with the planning group and therefore trusted their judgment on how to proceed.

The CEO announced this plan and introduced me as the person who would help assess the culture. He made it clear that this was to be considered important for the future of the sales force. It would be up to me in the various individual and group meetings to elicit and confront positive and negative feelings about the present culture and to raise the question about whether the future head of Sales should be an insider or outsider.

Over the next several months I met with groups of sales reps and discovered an almost unanimous support of the culture that had been built up. I wrote a report describing the culture and the strong sentiment to maintain it by promoting the insider

There was an interesting twist to these results about the culture itself. Everyone agreed that it was exceedingly hierarchical and that the VP of Sales had always called the shots of how sales should be approached. He not only issued goals, but had created a whole set of sales tools that he imposed on the reps. What made this acceptable was that once these tools were tried out, they worked well and made the reps' jobs easier. The reps also pointed out that the lower-level managers in the different regions encouraged some autonomy and innovation among the reps if they felt they could do things better. It was a delicate balance between authority and autonomy, but it worked well, and the reps did not want to see it changed.

The report was well received, and six months later, when the VP of Sales retired, they promoted the inside candidate with enthusiasm.

LESSONS

■ This case reinforced my belief that even if clients have a clear idea of the problem they are trying to solve, they do not necessarily have a clear or workable plan of how to solve it, and therefore need process help. I did not know anything about the problems of selling pharmaceuticals, but I did know how to assess a group's culture.

■ I confirmed again that using groups was the best way to decipher culture, because one very quickly discovers the central elements, the DNA of the culture so to speak. There were many elements to this organization's culture that were irrelevant to the succession issue. Individual interviews could not have brought this out in the way that a group discussion revealed it almost immediately.

CASE 18. Successfully Reducing Headquarters–Field Problems in the Internal Revenue Service

This project with the Internal Revenue Service (IRS) came about through my relationship with Dick Beckhard, who was my co-trainer in many workshops and became more of a mentor when he joined the Sloan School as a part-time

adjunct professor. Beckhard had a Level Two relationship
with the head of Training and Development of the IRS.

The commissioner of the IRS had noted that the *functional* commissioners who sat in Washington and reported
directly to the deputy commissioner (DC), who was a civil
servant (not a political appointee), were in constant battles
with the *regional* commissioners, who also reported to the
DC but were in many ways more autonomous in admin-
istering tax collection policy in their geographic regions.
The commissioner wanted the organization to work more
smoothly and asked the DC to find out what the problems
were and to develop a process to fix them.

The head of training was familiar with OD change management techniques, so he proposed the Beckhard process
to the DC. Beckhard himself was not available, but he
suggested me to implement it. The essence of this process
is to bring the right set of people into the room, in this case
all of the functional and regional commissioners with the
DC, and to engage them in the right kind of dialogue—a
dialogue that would seek consensus on how to handle the
problems that *they themselves had identified.*

Creating the agenda for this meeting required a trusted
outsider to gather the information, consolidate it, and
bring it to the meeting. Interviewing everyone around
the country was impractical, but a process of writing the
outside consultant a confidential letter in which each commissioner would outline his version of the problems and
what should be done about them had worked in similar
cases. The consultant would then summarize the issues
without identifying individual letter writers and present
those issues to the group meeting. The purpose was to get
early involvement of the participants and to ensure that the
meeting agenda was based on their own input.

I was brought on board as an outside consultant to pull together the content of the letters and to facilitate the full-day problem-solving meeting of all the commissioners and the DC. I first had to meet with the head of training, who was the "contact client," and fully work through the procedure with him, especially how to get the commissioners to write me honest letters about their issues. I then met the DC, who was the "primary client," and established a Level Two relationship with him that enabled him to write a sincere letter to the commissioners that this was his project, and if the full-day meeting was to have any value, they must feel free to tell me exactly what was on their minds. He assured them that I would not reveal their individual identities.

The DC then described this process to all the commissioners in person and asked for their feedback and agreement. Everyone agreed, the letters were sent to me, and I analyzed them and constructed an agenda for the meeting that would capture what were clearly the most pressing areas of conflict and the greatest opportunities for better coordination and collaboration. At the meeting of the total group, I opened the meeting with a review and clarification of the agenda document. The DC then took over to assure the group that this was his meeting and he wanted the group to work constructively.

I then went into a facilitator role to clarify issues, summarize occasionally, and test for consensus. By the end of the day, a whole new set of agreements had been made, the DC had been given some powerful feedback on how his management style was at times making headquarters–field issues worse, and the group parted with a much better sense of how to coordinate their efforts as a total organization. They decided on next steps, including having follow-up meetings of the total group to check on progress.

LESSONS

■ This worked because the whole adaptive process was planned jointly by an insider and an outsider consultant. The insider knew what would work, what kind of person the DC was; the outsider knew of a process of intervening to gather data that would enable the group to confront their problems. No step was taken without full insider involvement.

■ It was crucial that the DC, who was the "boss" and the primary client, understood and accepted the whole process, including that he would get some potentially painful feedback on his own style. It was up to me to forewarn him that if we went this route, he would have to get and accept feedback.

■ Most of the commissioners confirmed that what made it possible for them to write me honest letters was that the DC had convinced them that he wanted this meeting and wanted to create a more collaborative group. They trusted him, and therefore trusted me.

■ The meeting improved relationships among all the commissioners because their letters highlighted areas of interdependence that they had not noticed before. The fact that they had a whole day together allowed them to get to know one another better in a less formal context. The fact that they planned further meetings gave them an incentive to build their relationships with one another. My having read all the letters gave me a deeper insight into their problems of collaboration, which made it possible for me to facilitate the meeting more effectively.

■ Having the commissioners write me letters instead of having me go around to interview them was an innova-

tive way to save time and to get people to think carefully about what they really wanted to talk about at the
meeting. I felt that this process worked as well as it did
because from the beginning it was jointly owned by the
key members of the organization. They knew what they
were trying to do, it made sense to me, and we all understood what the goals were and how it would work.

■ My role was to manage the process at all stages. Though
I had a role in dealing with the content of the letters, I
very carefully tried to avoid content seduction by focusing
primarily on helping them have an effective meeting.

Summary and Conclusions

Humble Consulting is most likely to be helpful in restructuring the client's *thought process* in one or more of the following ways. The consultant can help the client (1) reformulate
the problem, (2) rethink what the client's own role should be,
and (3) rethink what the consultant should do. It is in these
process areas that help can occur exceptionally rapidly,
even in the very first conversation, because the reformula-
tion may make the client realize that she now knows what
to do. The consultant can help in suggesting a better use of
his services than what the client might have initially thought
about or suggested.

Clients rarely consider the power of working with the
consultant on all aspects of their situation, combining
the insider and outsider perspectives in figuring out what
is going on, what needs attention, and what to do about
it. The consultant can also help by developing a coaching
relationship with the client, what can best be thought of as
"role coaching" in that the consultant can help the client in
developing and implementing further adaptive moves. The

consultant must have empathy but carefully avoid content seduction because, as the outsider, he will never have the insider's direct knowledge of what will and will not work in the client's culture.

SUGGESTION FOR THE READER

Get together with a fellow consultant and review several recent cases from the point of view of what kind of *process* help you provided. Be very specific and give lots of examples so that you can learn from each other.

Alternatively, get together with a friend or spouse and discuss a recent decision that you made from a purely *process* point of view. How did you make the decision, were there alternative ways to do it, and how do you feel about how you did it?

SEVEN

The New Kinds of Adaptive Moves

In this final chapter I tackle some of the realities of helping with complex, messy problems, and flesh out a little more what it means to make an adaptive move, as contrasted with "major" diagnostic interventions or solutions designed either to solve the problem or build some specific skill. The adaptive move is not another "tool" in the consultant's bag and there are no formulas for "what to do when," because so much depends on the actual situational complexities, which include the personalities of the consultant and the client and the need to combine personalization and authenticity in building the relationship.

The Adaptive Move as Both Diagnosis and Intervention

In most consulting models, it is stated that interventions should be based on a diagnosis. Various forms of diagnosis are suggested, such as interviewing everyone, doing a diagnostic survey, or giving various diagnostic instruments to various parts of the client system to create typological categories or provide a profile of various diagnostic dimensions. This model works only if the client has identified a clear problem and has worked out with the consultant what dimensions are relevant and what kind of remedy might be helpful. If we accept the presumption that organizational problems are increasingly complex, messy, and unstable, then it is likely that such a diagnostic process will at the minimum waste time and at the maximum do unanticipated harm.

I think such problems are especially likely in the area of *culture diagnosis*, where a survey of individual perceptions creates a typology based on clusters of such intercorrelated perceptions and is then given a name and treated as a category to be compared with other categories. Culture at its deeper levels is a shared group phenomenon that can be described and understood but not measured quantitatively. Only if the client and consultant have a Level Two joint understanding of the culture issues that they are grappling with would it be appropriate to consider "measuring" some elements of the culture.

The alternative to the diagnose, analyze, and recommend model is to work out with the client an adaptive move that will simultaneously reveal some diagnostic information and constitute an initial intervention. Often that first move is conversational, to help the client figure out what is really bothering him, locate what is the immediate organizational problem that is a source of worry, and then jointly develop the next adaptive move, where the word *adaptive* reminds us that there is no single problem to be identified and the word *move* reminds us that there is no master plan solution. Once we know what is really worrying the client, together we can begin to figure out the next move, which may be some further small intervention.

If we think of *moves*, we are accepting the reality that

every move will change the situation and reveal some new information. We then realize that diagnosis and intervention are, in fact, two sides of the same coin, and both processes occur with every move we make.

This way of thinking does not preclude planning big interventions, but it does presume that the consultant and client have correctly identified what is really worrying the client and what kind of big intervention might help reduce that worry. If the client is clear what kinds of changes need to be made, big diagnostic steps and programs of retraining, restructuring, and redesign of processes may be entirely appropriate, but only when carefully considered in terms of possible unanticipated consequences. Such consideration often reveals the need to become innovative, to get different people into the room to consider the issue and needed changes, and to change the conversation toward more of a dialogue. Innovative adaptive moves are an especially important concept in the safety field, as the following cases illustrate.

CASE 19. Safety Issues in Alpha Power

The traditional way that organizations deal with safety reviews after a serious accident is to go through linear processes of identifying "root causes," finding someone or something to blame, and then instituting new procedures and rules to ensure that that particular thing will never happen again. The problem is that in the search for the root cause, the organization is likely to overlook that the situation just before the accident was a complex, messy one and that there generally is no root cause, only an unfortunate combination of circumstances.

PCBS IN A DAMAGED TRANSFORMER

One of Alpha's transformers was hit by lightning and leaked its oil into the neighborhood, causing fires that required immediate attention. The engineer in charge of that transformer had regularly tested the transformer oil for PCBs (polychlorinated biphenyl), the dangerous carcinogenic chemical, and "knew" there were none in the oil, yet when he tested the oil on the ground right after the explosion, it showed high PCB levels. He did not want to cause unnecessary alarm, so he immediately sent several samples to the lab to check his readings.

This all happened just before Labor Day when the lab was closed. As a result, the company did not learn until a week later that the PCB levels were indeed extremely high, which meant that the firemen and other rescue personnel had been exposed for several days to these chemicals. The company was again hit with fines and bad publicity for "once again covering up environmental pollution."

Alpha already had a rule that all spills were to be reported immediately, but the engineer, being true to the engineering culture principle that one should check one's data before leaping into action and one should not cause unnecessary panic, had acted appropriately from his point of view. The mystery of the PCBs was not unraveled until six months later, when it was finally discovered that this transformer had been built twenty-five years earlier, when PCBs had not yet been labeled as dangerous and, in any case, were contained in *sealed* rods used for sound dampening that the lightning had accidentally ruptured.

My role in the aftermath was "educational," to support the idea that the engineer had acted entirely according to what we would expect in the engineering culture and to suggest that there was no point in trying to find fault with

him or with the lab but to shift the attention to the "worry"
that the environmental agencies continued to deeply mis-
trust the company in spite of the many positive environmental, health, and safety programs that were in place and
were working. I helped them to redefine the problem that
Alpha really had to work on showing the public and the
regulators that they were working hard to improve things,
even though accidents will continue to happen.

These insights led to two adaptive moves: (1) Reinforcing
the rule that was on the books to report all spills immediately, no matter whether you think they are dangerous or
not; and (2) starting a program of inviting regulators and
staff of the local Environmental Protection Agency into
company meetings on a regular basis to see what safety
and environmental programs were being pursued. Over
several years this second program produced important
results in that even if another accident happened, the regulators knew that the company was doing its best to reduce
the impact.

LESSONS

■ The big lesson here was to shift the focus from the
immediate analysis and blame process to the realization
that the real worry was the negative view that the regulators had of Alpha's efforts, leading to an innovative adaptive move of bringing the regulators into the organization
to let them see what the company's programs were.

THE ALPHA TIME-OUT PROGRAM

Upward communication is one of the biggest problems, not
only in the field of safety but also in maintaining product or
service quality. Alpha had for years announced to employees that if they observed a safety problem on the job, they

were to request that the job stop until a safety expert could come to declare that it was safe. But it was awkward for employees to speak up, so the company created a credit-card-sized "time-out card" that an employee could pull out and thereby declare a job stoppage. All employees were trained in when and how to use the card and encouraged to use it. The company was quite proud of this program, and the employees were happy to have a way of expressing their safety concerns.

The program was several years old when, in our regular focus groups with employees, we found that it was working very unevenly and was considered a problem in some groups. What had happened? Because the program was working so well, the director of safety and others in senior management realized that this was an important data source for determining what kinds of safety problems were occurring, a very important thing to know in terms of allocating scarce funds to various kinds of maintenance issues in this old system. To gather this information, the company set up a program for the middle managers just above the supervisors of the work crews to fill out a brief form for each time-out explaining what the safety problem was. These forms would initially be filled out by the supervisors, collected and analyzed by the middle managers, and then sent up to headquarters for further analysis.

Middle managers noticed that the number of time-outs over a period of months varied greatly among the supervisors under them. So, like "good managers," they asked the supervisors who had a lot of time-outs "What's going on in your crew; why are you having so many time-outs?" They did not realize that this question would embarrass many supervisors and would inevitably lead to some supervisors sending signals to the work crews that they were wimps and were taking advantage of the program by calling time-outs all the time. That unanticipated consequence damaged the program in unknown ways and made it necessary to now find a new adaptive move to overcome the newfound hesitancy to identify and report safety problems!

LESSONS

- In complex human systems, it is often exceedingly difficult to predict how a well-intentioned program will have unforeseen consequences. Even with all the pilot programs that had been done, there was no way of knowing that middle managers would now have information about the relative effectiveness of their various supervisors and work crews, and that their use of this knowledge would undermine getting the very information that the system was designed to collect. I had encountered a very similar situation in an international elevator organization, where a centralized maintenance organization was required to clear all work in order to standardize and maintain high quality in the operation. This made it possible for senior management to locate which countries had the most problems and inquire about the cause of the problems. They later discovered that those countries reacted to the inquiries by no longer reporting maintenance issues to headquarters, shifting maintenance to local organizations and thereby undermining the original purpose of maintaining a high-quality centralized system.

- The new worry to be addressed was how to avoid having a safety information system become a managerial control system. This would require bringing together the designers, managers, and employees to have a new conversation to figure out what to do next that would honor both sets of needs.

CASE 20. Reducing the Number of Deaths in the US Forest Service

A different kind of messy problem is how to reduce deaths among firefighters in the US Forest Service. I am currently working as a shadow consultant with one of their internal consultant/analysts who is trying to get management away from "root cause analysis" and "finding the person to blame." Instead, how can one get work crews to recognize and accept the messiness in forest fires and develop group-based adaptive moves to avoid lethal dangers? My academic colleague Karl Weick has been arguing for some time that in these situations one needs "*group* sense making," in that no individual will be able to see the whole picture and know where danger might be coming from (Weick, 1995; Weick and Sutcliffe, 2007).

Rules and procedures can never cover all the unexpected contingencies that arise, and no individual supervisor can see enough of the situation to make valid decisions. The needed adaptive move is to find a way for the group to share what they see and enable a collective response. But the individual firefighter's perception is narrowed by the need to give full attention to the immediate task. The interesting innovative adaptive move that my colleague is proposing to the Forest Service is that when a crew is out fighting a forest fire, there should always be a designated observer who steps back, tries to take in the whole situation, and keeps reporting information to the group as a whole for sense making before action is taken.

That observer role could be rotated so that all the firefighters would get training in observing the whole scene.

As we continue to talk, I am learning that the Forest Service, as a culture, has subcultures within it that operate from different assumptions: is the core mission of the firefighting organization to fight fire, to preserve property, to save lives, or even to aid conservation with allowing controlled burns? The implication is that any so-called solution, like group sense-making, runs into different responses from different contingencies with different goals and tacit assumptions. The problem now shifts from "What kind of solution will save lives?" to "What next step do we need to take to get the firefighting organization itself to look into a mirror and examine its own assumptions and organization?" If and when that step is taken, there will be a new group of insiders who can begin to work on the next adaptive move to make.

LESSONS

■ The lesson here is that a new kind of innovative adaptive move has first to be seen as appropriate by the power structure of the organization as something "better" than the current procedure, leading to a whole series of new conversations and training moves by the internal consultant with the executives who want change and with insiders in the group that is expected to make changes. Here again, it seems that getting the right people into the room and stimulating a new kind of conversation becomes a crucial move. It also reinforces once again that some of the most important work by the consultant is to help the client understand the true messiness of the problem, that old solutions will no longer work, and that new sets of problem solvers and new kinds of dialogic conversations are initially the most important moves. As the previous chapter highlighted, the main changes are to develop new processes for how to define and work on a problem.

CASE 21. Helping INPO Provide Better Help in Working with Nuclear Plants

This case is especially interesting because in my advisory role I was helping the helpers. INPO's job is to visit nuclear plants on an annual schedule, analyze their operations, identify problems, and offer help in solving those problems. The unexpected issue was that even though INPO is funded by the plants to help the plants to be safe, plant managements to varying degrees resist having external evaluations and get quite defensive about some of the findings of the INPO analyses.

I found myself talking a lot about the human problems of "helping" and suggested that *how to help* was as important or even more important than figuring out the safety problems. In fact, when I asked some of the analysts how long it took them on a site visit to figure out what the main problems were, they said "about a half day," because the important safety problems derived from visible managerial and interpersonal issues.

However, in the engineering culture, such insights had no validity, so it often took the entire length of the one-week visit to convert those insights into measures and written documents. That part of the process was well embedded, but the manner of providing feedback to plant and site management provided opportunities to redesign the process to make the feedback less threatening. Though it was applied unevenly, the essence of the new adaptive way of reporting findings was to work on building Level Two relationships between the INPO analysts and the employees and managers of the plant

LESSONS

■ When you throw safety into the mix with productivity, scheduling, and the human desire to be efficient, it is easy to say "safety is number 1," but observations of what goes on even in high-hazard industries belies this espoused value. What makes safety a complex, messy problem is that it is always traded off against other values (Amalberti, 2013). In INPO this showed up in the complex management structures of power company sites that contained nuclear as well as coal-fired plants. Some of the defensiveness of nuclear plant management was produced by the pressure from corporate management to be efficient and cost conscious. One of INPO's important tactical problems, therefore, was when and how to involve site management in the feedback sessions. As I look back on my five years on the Advisory Committee, my most important contribution was to shift their problem-solving attention from how to be better analysts to how to be better helpers.

Changing the Nature of the Conversation: Innovative Adaptive Moves

I conclude this chapter with several cases that strike me as examples of thinking more innovatively about adaptive moves and interventions. The theme continues to be how to find out what the client is worried about, what the client really wants, what problems the client needs to address. The most important adaptive moves are often the early ones that help the client figure out the answers to these questions.

CASE 22. Successful and Failed Adaptive Moves— DEC's Strategy Revisited

DEC in the 1980s was wildly successful, but changes in the technology, in the market for computers, and in its internal dynamics created a series of tremendously messy problems (Schein, 2003). The changes in the technology made the design of computers more complicated, requiring more collaboration between various engineering groups and software. Ken Olsen's managerial style of empowering people worked well in a young, innovative organization creating new products but became dysfunctional when, with success, age, and growth, products were created by large groups that became powerful and became destructively competitive with one another.

The culture of DEC was built around innovation, and because the early products were successful, the absence of a strong "business gene" in its DNA allowed personnel and other costs to get out of control. Because growth had always taken care of cost problems, Ken strongly resisted laying off people; they were, in a sense, his children, and his loyalty to his people had been one of DEC's strengths.

One of the many paradoxes of the DEC story is that they did not lack insight. Ken and his managers could see all the changes externally and internally, but they could not develop adaptive moves, relying instead on their faith in innovation and continued growth. Business analysts and outside consultants could not understand how DEC could fail to see the market moving toward small, easy-to-use desktop computers. The point is that they did see it and chose not to respond, counting instead on their trusted sophisticated consumers to provide a big enough market to continue to grow. DEC qualified in the late 1980s as a complex, messy problem. I was working with many internal OD consultants who had been hired by the various units within DEC. We had many joint meetings to figure out how best to help the company, but when there are strong personal forces at work among key executives, it becomes harder and harder to make effective adaptive moves.

One successful move concerned Ken's emotional outbursts. Ken's upsets often led to verbally punishing selected executives in front of others, a process that everyone hated but could not stop. I helped the Operations Committee deal with Ken's rants by offering the hypothesis that he got angry when something made him *anxious*. If the group could sense his growing anxiety, they quickly gave Ken data that things were under control, which did indeed reduce the number of outbursts. This was, in a certain sense, my clearest example of an adaptive move. We could not change Ken directly, but the group could change itself in how it dealt with Ken, which, in turn, did change his behavior somewhat.

I was also still working with the Operations Committee and the senior VP of Human Resources, whom Ken trusted completely, trying to work out year by year how to help Ken steer what became an increasingly strong group of "barons" running their own empires. The Woods Meetings became an important part of the governance structure, because it was at those meetings where Ken sought consensus on what to do next. Those meetings often included outsiders as resources to stimulate the group's thinking and to present a point of view that Ken wanted to emphasize or that other senior executives thought to be essential for Ken to hear. In one of those meetings in the late 1980s, Ken told the organizer, Sue, "We really need to look at our product strategy at the next Woods Meeting," which was a clear indication that Ken knew that they needed to focus but did not know how to make it happen.

To avoid a destructive fight at the meeting, Sue and I agreed that the best move would be to get a world-class strategy professor, the late Sumantra Ghoshal, who was known and liked by DEC, to come to the meeting, give some conceptual input, and then run an exercise that would lead to some strategic focus. The participants would be all the key senior executives, which, of course, included the three proponents of the product options that had been proposed. My role was to brief Sumantra on the depth and messiness of the problem and help out during the Woods Meeting in whatever way I could.

The meeting took place deep in the Maine woods at Ken's retreat, which included a general building for meetings and meals, five small cabins that could each house four to six people, and various recreational facilities. It was set on a small lake below a mountain and could only be reached via a logging road from a town six hours away or by helicopter from the nearest town with an airstrip. We all flew up in a six-person jet, which shuttled back and forth between Boston and this small town, then helicoptered for a half hour to the retreat. The meeting usually consisted of an intense morning and early afternoon, a time for major recreation for the rest of the afternoon, and a meeting after dinner. People were encouraged to take a hike up the mountain, go canoeing, play horseshoes or volleyball, and enjoy themselves. Ken wanted people to do things together, become mutually trusting, and reach a workable consensus.

My role at these retreats was usually to hang around close to Ken to give him an opportunity to express his thoughts and frustrations to me in private. I mostly listened to what often turned into long rants about various people who were not doing what Ken hoped they would do. Whenever possible, I tried to provide perspective, giving possible reasons why they might be doing what they were doing, suggesting alternative ways of thinking about the issues, and making occasional suggestions to go talk to others in the company whom he trusted instead of just stewing about it. Having done this for many years, I realized that Ken had very few confidants, and my role was not to make suggestions, though occasionally I did that, but mostly to provide Ken an opportunity to sort out his own thinking. After his rants he often said he now knew what he wanted to do.

At the retreat Sumantra made a heroic effort to show the need for focus in a situation where excessive costs and limited resources made it impossible to pursue all three major product developments: a new large computer system called Aquarius, the Alpha chip, and AltaVista, the new search engine. The discussion was spirited, and everyone agreed in principle, but I could see, both at the meeting and in the subsequent months, that each of the three product champions was as convinced as ever that *he* was the solution to DEC's future. Ken even had the illusion that some consensus had been reached, but what he did not see or could not grasp was that the fighting between the barons had turned ugly, with alleged lying to one another, exaggerating claims, minimizing technological problems, and allegedly stealing resources from one another in various underhanded ways. Had Ken been a different kind of personality, he might have fired all three, but these were his "children." He respected their intellectual power, and deep down he did not want to see them as ordinary mortals in serious competition with one another.

Various members of the Operations Committee and of the board worked on finding adaptive moves that would get the situation under control, but in the early 1990s, the struggle got worse. Ken increasingly lost control until the board forced him to retire. The board then put a more dictatorial person in charge and set about to "fix" the company, which many believed was basically to get it ready for sale.

LESSONS

■ The most important lesson of my many years of consulting with DEC was to realize that certain constellations of complex, messy problems cannot be fixed or even ameliorated because different parts of the client system have evolved fundamentally different goals and values. I learned that with success, growth, and age, the constellation of forces in the system changes in unanticipated ways. When I am asked why DEC failed, even with all my consulting help, the only tongue-in-cheek answer I can give is "They might have failed even sooner if I and other helpers had not been there."

CASE 23. Creating a Different Kind of Conversation in Saab Combitech

An example of different people having a different kind of conversation from the usual problem-solving discussion was a workshop that I co-designed with the head of Saab Combitech, the technical division of Saab, which consisted of six research units, each working for a different division of the company. My client, Per Risberg, wanted me to design an activity that would help the heads of these research units recognize the potential of collaborating instead of functioning as independent units. After much conversation Per and I decided that the three-day meeting should be divided into several segments.

In segment 1 I would explain the concept of culture and how to decipher it. Each group would then designate two of its members to become "ethnographers," who would, in segment 2, go into one another's groups to learn about one another's cultures, and then, in segment 3, would report out their findings to the total group. They could then, in segment 4, collectively discuss where there were cultural themes that the groups had in common that could serve as the basis for developing more collaboration. The impact of observing one another with a cultural lens and being forced to talk to one another about what they observed created a completely different kind of conversation that led to many forms of collaboration over the next few years.

LESSONS

- What made this work was the joint design with the leader of the group. He understood what he wanted and was very happy to co-create the adaptive move with me, in this case a "big intervention" in the process of how the groups interacted. He also understood that he owned the intervention and made his needs the driving force. The high degree of personalization between him and me made this whole experience one of my most satisfying and successful consultations.

CASE 24. The Use of Dialogue in Shell's Exploration and Production Division

Dialogic conversations are especially relevant to situations that are open-ended and complex, because the dialogue format is premised on thinking together to find common ground to figure out what to do, not to make a quick diagnosis or decision. An interesting example occurred in my working with the Exploration and Production Division of Shell Oil Company to help them decipher their culture and figure out how they wanted to be measured. After a day discussing the work of this unit and the cultural assumptions on which it was built, we found ourselves unable to reach any kind of agreement on how the unit should be measured. It was an off-site meeting, so I knew I had the opportunity to use the after-dinner time for further discussion.

When the twelve of us were settled, I said, "I would like to try something different tonight. I would like us to go around the room and have each one of us, one at a time and without questions or interruptions, tell us how you individually would like to be measured and what the concept of measurement means to you."

The group agreed, so for the next half hour or so we listened as each of us revealed his (they were all men) personal concept of how he wanted to be measured and learned, in that process, what the key cultural dimension was that we had not been able to identify in our general discussion. The members of the exploration group all wanted to be measured on their courage in taking risks to find new oil deposits. They wanted to be rewarded for *risk taking*. The production group members wanted to be rewarded for safely managing the extraction process, which involved anticipating and avoiding as many safety risks as possible. They wanted to be rewarded for *risk avoidance*. As obvious as this sounds in retrospect, it was significant that the group could not identify this issue until I suggested the dialogic form of analyzing what we each meant by "measurement."

LESSONS

■ As problems become more complex and messy, the deciphering of "What is the problem?" "What is worrying us?" "What should we be trying to change?" itself becomes more complex and messy. Our psychological need to make sense of things leads to oversimplifying, to wanting the comfort of knowing the "root cause," of wanting the sense of progress that comes with "identifying and working the problem," of "knowing what to do." Yet clarity may come only when we acknowledge that we don't know what to do. So let's return to the situation I described at the beginning of this book—consulting with the academic medical center lunch group.

CASE 25. The Ad Hoc Lunch Group in the Academic Medical Center

This case is currently evolving and is therefore the right place to think further about adaptive moves. Next month, I am again meeting with this group of doctor administrators and the COO of this academic medical center for our sixth lunch meeting, and I again don't know what to do. But I can reflect on what moves I have made and build up my confidence that in that meeting I will find something useful to do.

At the first meeting, we did a check-in to say who each of us is and why he or she had come to the lunch. The common theme was curiosity and a desire to get new ideas to keep the hospital's improvement program moving forward. The COO's agenda was to find a way to get more of the key players in the system to begin to be "on the same page" in terms of improvement goals.

As I listened to the group, I found that they often used

concepts quite loosely and inconsistently, especially the concept of *culture*. I found myself interrupting from time to time to ask for examples and then clarifying by explaining my model of culture, playing the role of expert, and being authentic. I noted that there were important subcultures represented in the group that were not fully understood, so I asked a provocative question: "If you are the head of the hospital, what is your worst nightmare?" to which the answer was "An unwarranted patient death." I then asked: "If you are the dean of the medical school, what is your worst nightmare?" to which the answer was "A researcher falsifying his research results and being found out, thus totally embarrassing the university." Very different responses reflecting very different goals.

A move that worked at the next meeting was to listen to the various members for the amount of emotional energy that each comment conveyed and then to steer the conversation to focus on that comment. One late arrival had just come from a frustrating set of events in the operating room, so I suggested that we talk further about his experience and found this to lead to several possible changes that the group thought of that could be made in their procedures. I observed that most of these ideas were extremely large changes in fundamental procedures of how resources were allocated, which led me to try another "educational move." I gave a very brief description of the need to think in terms of *small changes* that are doable and have big consequences instead of large changes that may not be implementable at all. I did not know what such changes might be in the hospital environment but gave some personal examples of what I meant.

In the next meeting I asked the group how the members felt about what we were doing and learned that most of them enjoyed the unstructured opportunity to get together and talk. They noted that in their work lives they were so overloaded that there were no opportunities to just get together, talk, and share views. Our work ethic does not provide permission or an excuse to just get together and talk.

The most significant lesson in all this may well be that the key adaptive move was the COO's decision to ask me as an outsider to meet with a volunteer group to talk about culture change over lunch. Bringing a new group together over lunch to have a new kind of dialogic conversation may well be one of those small changes that could have significant long-range payoff as more of the doctor administrators form relationships with one another and get some clarity around the complex, messy problems they are dealing with.

I have learned not to worry about not knowing what to do. As this group builds, one or the other of us will figure out what to do, because we are becoming more open and trusting with one another. That is, to me, the most important outcome.

Summary and Conclusions

In this chapter I have focused on the nature and variety of what I have called "adaptive moves." By calling them "adaptive," I am emphasizing that they are not solutions to "the problem" but actions intended to improve the situation and elicit more diagnostic data for the planning of the next move. By calling them "moves," I am again emphasizing that they are small efforts to improve the situation, not grand plans or huge interventions.

I have observed that such adaptive moves often provide immediate and effective help, leading to an entirely different concept of what the consultant should be doing—focusing on what is worrying the client and helping the client figure out what the two of you together might consider to do next.

Given the growing complexity of organizational life and the increasing speed at which everything is happening, the best metaphor for adaptive moves is Improvisation Theater. I have learned that plans, structures, rules, and routines can make us comfortable, but, in the end, they may not be helpful. On the other hand, getting personal, building relationships, and joint improvisation seem to work better for fast, real help.

SUGGESTION FOR THE READER

Get together with two or more colleagues who want to explore with you what it might mean in the work setting or at home to think about introducing a new kind of conversation, or trying to have a different kind of personal relationship with one another or your boss or your partners. Don't look for answers. Allow yourselves to mindfully and creatively explore new small changes in your own life around those concerns that are messiest and most worrisome.

Let go of formulas and tools. See if you can capture your own spirit of inquiry and enhance your curiosity. Remember that the purpose of dialogue is to explore an issue, not to reach a conclusion. At the end of the dialogue you may still not know what to do, but you will have a deeper understanding of the complexity of the problems you have talked about.

Concluding Comments—Some Final Thoughts on How to Be Really Helpful

I can summarize and conclude my argument best with several propositions that I have tried to explain throughout. These are a restatement of the working propositions I articulated in Chapter 2. It is the *combination* of all of these thoughts that ultimately defines Humble Consulting:

- To be really helpful requires locating what the real problem is, that is, what is worrying the client while accepting the fact that there is no "real problem," only a set of worries that may be all over the map.

- To locate what is worrying the client requires open and trusting communication between client and helper. The client has to feel secure enough to reveal what is personally bothering him or her.

- To facilitate open and trusting communication requires building a Level Two personal relationship that goes beyond the formal Level One professional relationship of most helping situations.

- Building a Level Two working relationship requires personalizing the relationship through conveying an attitude, from the moment of first contact, of "commitment to helping," "curiosity," and "caring for the client and the situation."

■ Personalization occurs through some combination of asking more-personal questions, listening empathetically both for the situation and the client's feelings about it, and/or revealing more-personal thoughts and spontaneous reactions.

■ Once a Level Two working relationship is felt, the definition of the problem, where help is really needed, and what might be done next then becomes a joint ongoing dialogue between helper and client.

■ If the problem turns out to be simple and clear, the helper can go into the expert or doctor role, if appropriate, or refer the client to an expert or doctor. If the problem turns out to be complex and messy, the client and helper figure out a feasible **adaptive move,** knowing that this may not **solve** the problem but will help and will reveal new information on the basis of which to figure out the **next adaptive move.**

■ These have to be joint decisions, because the consultant will never know enough about the client's personal situation or organizational culture to make a recommendation, and the client will never know enough about all the consequences of a given intervention such as surveys or other diagnostic process tools to unilaterally decide on a given action.

■ It is therefore one of the consultant's responsibilities to understand the consequences of different kinds of adaptive moves and to fully brief the client about those consequences to determine whether or not the client is ready for that move.

What all of these points have in common is that they derive from commitment, curiosity, and caring built on an attitude of humility in the face of a client who needs to feel honored and cared for, and humility in the face of the complexity and messiness of the situations that the client faces. What is most new and different? The need to *personalize* and the emphasis on *curiosity* as the most important driver of the whole process.

So Where Do We Go from Here? The Broader Implications

I conclude with an important but frightening thought. This new model of consulting is, of course, a broader model of the helping process in general. Parents will be more effective in their parenting if they practice a bit of Humble Consulting. Service people will be more effective in selling and solving problems, as, for example, the Apple helpers at the Genius Bar have learned. Doctors, lawyers, and other professionals will provide better help if they become humble consultants. But, most of all, leaders and managers at all levels will find that they must from time to time adopt this role in order to produce quality and safety in their fundamental organizational processes.

This will be most difficult for leaders and managers, because they are always supposed to know what to do, to have the vision, to be able to tell others what to do, to be the hero. Yet they will encounter more and more problems and situations in which they won't know what to do. The most important learning for them will be to accept that it is okay not to know what to do. You then get the right people in the room, most likely some of your subordinates, create a dialogue, and together figure out the best next adaptive move.

What is most frightening about this is the discovery that so few leaders and managers realize that they also will, like consultants, encounter situations where they will not know what to do. Hopefully, they will learn that even for a leader it is okay not to know what to do, and move forward from there.

References

Amalberti, R. (2013) *Navigating Safety*. Dordrech, Germany: Springer.

Barrett, F. J. (2012) *Yes to the Mess: Surprising Leadership Lessons from Jazz*. Cambridge, MA: Harvard Business School Press.

Bohm, D. (1989) *On Dialogue*. Ojai, CA: David Bohm Seminars.

Bushe, G. R., and R. J. Marshak, eds. (2015) *Dialogic Organization Development*. San Francisco: Berrett-Koehler.

Goffman, E. (1959) *The Presentation of Self in Everyday Life*. New York: Doubleday Anchor.

———. (1963) *Behavior in Public Places*. New York: Free Press.

———. (1967) *Interaction Ritual*. New York: Pantheon.

Heifetz, R. A. (1994) *Leadership without Easy Answers*. Cambridge, MA: Harvard University Press.

Isaacs, W. (1999) *Dialogue*. New York: Doubleday Currency.

Langer, E. (1997) *The Power of Mindful Learning*. Reading, MA: Addison-Wesley.

Madanes, C. (1981) *Strategic Family Therapy*. San Francisco: Jossey-Bass.

Plsek, P. (2014) *Accelerating Health Care Transformation with Lean and Innovation*. Boca Raton, FL: CRC Press, Taylor & Francis Group.

Scharmer, C. O. (2007) *Theory U*. Cambridge, MA: SoL Press.

Schein, E. H. (1969) *Process Consultation*. Reading, MA: Addison-Wesley.

———. (1999) *Process Consultation Revisited*. Englewood Cliffs, NJ: Prentice-Hall.

———. (2003) *DEC Is Dead; Long Live DEC*. San Francisco: Berrett-Koehler.

———. (2009) *Helping*. San Francisco: Berrett-Koehler.

————. (2010) *Organizational Culture and Leadership.* 4th ed. San Francisco: Jossey-Bass, Wiley.

————. (2013) *Humble Inquiry.* San Francisco: Berrett-Koehler.

Schein, E. H., and W. G. Bennis. (1965) *Personal and Organizational Change through Group Methods.* New York: Wiley.

Schein, E. H., and J. Van Maanen (2014) *Career Anchors.* 4th ed. San Francisco: Wiley.

Senge, P. (1990) *The Fifth Discipline.* New York: Doubleday.

Weick, K. E. (1995) *Sensemaking in Organizations.* Thousand Oaks, CA: Sage.

Weick, K. E., and K. M. Sutcliffe. (2007) *Managing the Unexpected.* 2nd ed. San Francisco: Jossey-Bass, Wiley.

Acknowledgments

Many colleagues and clients have influenced the writing of this book. On the colleague side I owe a special thanks to Gervase Bushe who first convinced me a couple of years ago to pay attention to *Dialogic Organization Development* and to Otto Scharmer whose *Theory U* also opened the door to thinking about help and consultation differently. The actual writing, the only real test of whether you "know" something or not, was greatly helped by my many conversations with my son Peter and my editor Steven Piersanti.

In building up the ideas I benefitted greatly from intense generative conversations with David Bradford, Noam Cook, Philip Mix, and Jo Sanzgiri. I have gotten important ideas and feedback from my son Peter, with whom I am planning to write the next book—*Humble Leadership*. Other colleagues and friends who tested the validity of these ideas with me were Rosa Carrillo, John Cronkite, Tina Doerffer, Mary Jane Kornacki, Tim Kuppler, Joichi Ogawa, Diane Rawlins, Jack Silversin, Tony Suchman, and Ilene Wasserman. Many others who helped me sort this out in conversations were Manisha Bajal, Kathryn Schuyler Goldman, Mei Lin Fung, Kimberly Wiefling, Lily and Peter Chen, and Marjory Godfrey. I know I have forgotten some other important helpers and I apologize profusely to them.

Ideas get worked out in presentations, which leads me

to thank Jeff Richardson and the South Bay Organization Development Network for opportunities to present this new way of thinking about the helping process to a sympathetic and yet potentially critical audience.

And, of course, the unsung heroes of this book are the clients with whom I have worked who not only presented the messy problems but whose involvement with me in figuring out what to do taught me the essential components of this new way of working.

Index

About the Author— in His Own Words

I came into the world of "real work" from an academic background— a general education at the University of Chicago, a Masters Degree in Social Psychology from Stanford, and a PhD in Social Psychology, which included sociology and anthropology, from Harvard's Department of Social Relations. I planned to be an experimental social psychologist but decided after a productive postdoctoral stint at the Walter Reed Institute of Research to try my hand at doing this kind of research in the MIT Sloan School of Management. I had no idea at the time I made this decision in 1956 that the world of management would not only expose me to a different kind of student with different aspirations but would also provide opportunities for consulting with real organizations on real-life consequential issues and problems about which I knew nothing.

But my training as a scientist also made me a learner. It is in writing this book that I have become aware of the importance of curiosity and what we called in the early days of organization development "the spirit of inquiry," which is, of course, the very basis of science. I found consulting to be both fascinating and troubling. We were out there getting paid to help, but the models of consulting that I read about rarely seemed to apply to what clients confronted me with. Rather than forcing my practice into the existing models, I found it more important to document what I was experiencing and figure out what I was learning from these experiences. It was at these times that I found sociology and anthropology to be crucial sources of theory and concepts.

I also learned that in the human sciences, experimentation was not feasible. The very act of doing research, of inquiring as part of a helping process, was intervening in and changing the very process we were observing. But, being trained as a scientist, I found that observing, documenting, and trying to make sense of our experiences was in this domain "good science." I often thought that in the human arena we are still at the Darwinian stage of observing, documenting, and trying out various concepts and theories, but we have not yet found a master set of integrative concepts that explain it all. In the search for those concepts, the best we can do is to tell our colleagues what we have observed in our various experiences and what sense we can make of those observations. We put it out there as our "conclusions," knowing full well that these are only our current hypotheses to be discarded, accepted, or elaborated on by the next generation of observers and sense makers. It is in this spirit that I feel I can say "This is how the helping process works," and therefore "This is what you should do when you are trying to help."

This process has worked so far in that I have gotten Lifetime Achievement Awards as a Scholar/Practitioner from the Academy of Management and in Organization

Development from the International OD Network. But the learning process is never finished.

Working in Silicon Valley has focused me on a new issue—how leadership has evolved in this high-speed world of innovation and has led inevitably to what will be my next project—a book entitled *Humble Leadership.* I will co-author this with my son Peter, who has had multiple experiences of leading and managing in the hothouse of Silicon Valley and has discovered with me how very messy the problems of tomorrow's organizations will really be and how unrealistic most of today's proposed models of leadership really are. I think of each book as my "final statement," only to find that I keep encountering new things that I feel I have to observe, document, and try to make sense of.

Also by Edgar H. Schein

Humble Inquiry
The Gentle Art of Asking Instead of Telling

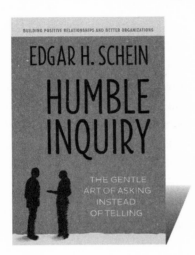

Communication is essential in a healthy organization. But all too often when we interact with people—especially those who report to us—we simply tell them what we think they need to know. This shuts them down. To generate bold new ideas, to avoid disastrous mistakes, to develop agility and flexibility, we need to practice Humble Inquiry.

Ed Schein defines Humble Inquiry as "the fine art of drawing someone out, of asking questions to which you do not know the answer, of building a relationship based on curiosity and interest in the other person." In this bestselling book, Schein contrasts Humble Inquiry with other kinds of inquiry, shows the benefits Humble Inquiry provides, and offers advice on overcoming the cultural, organizational, and psychological barriers that keep us from practicing it.

Paperback, 144 pages, ISBN 978-1-60994-981-5
PDF ebook, ISBN 978-1-60994-982-2

Berrett–Koehler Publishers, Inc.
www.bkconnection.com   **800.929.2929**

Helping
How to Offer, Give, and Receive Help

Edgar Schein analyzes the social and psychological dynamics common to all types of helping relationships, explains why help is often not helpful, and shows what any would-be helpers must do to ensure that their assistance is both welcomed and genuinely useful.

"Schein provides many anecdotes from his consulting practice, and his short, practical book is rich in insights."
—**Harvard Business Review**

Paperback, 192 pages, ISBN 978-1-60509-856-2
PDF ebook, ISBN 978-1-57675-872-4

With Peter S. DeLisi, Paul J. Kampas, and Michael M. Sonduck

DEC Is Dead, Long Live DEC
The Lasting Legacy of Digital Equipment Corporation

Digital Equipment Corporation was one of the pioneering companies of the computer age, yet it ultimately failed. In a real-life story that reads like a classical tragedy, Schein—who was a high-level consultant to DEC for forty years—and his coauthors show that the very culture responsible for DEC's rise ultimately led to its downfall.

Paperback, 336 pages, ISBN 978-1-57675-305-7
PDF ebook, ISBN 978-1-60509-408-3

Berrett–Koehler Publishers, Inc.
www.bkconnection.com   **800.929.2929**

Berrett–Koehler
Publishers

Connecting people and ideas
to create a world that works for all

Dear Reader,

Thank you for picking up this book and joining our worldwide community of Berrett-Koehler readers. We share ideas that bring positive change into people's lives, organizations, and society.

To welcome you, we'd like to offer you a free e-book. You can pick from among twelve of our bestselling books by entering the promotional code **BKP92E** here: http://www.bkconnection.com/welcome.

When you claim your free e-book, we'll also send you a copy of our e-newsletter, the *BK Communiqué*. Although you're free to unsubscribe, there are many benefits to sticking around. In every issue of our newsletter you'll find

- A free e-book
- Tips from famous authors
- Discounts on spotlight titles
- Hilarious insider publishing news
- A chance to win a prize for answering a riddle

Best of all, our readers tell us, "Your newsletter is the only one I actually read." So claim your gift today, and please stay in touch!

Sincerely,

Charlotte Ashlock
Steward of the BK Website

Questions? Comments? Contact me at bkcommunity@bkpub.com.